9/21

JOHN R. DONAHUE, S.J.

WHAT DOES THE LORD REQUIRE?

*A Bibliographical Essay on the Bible
and Social Justice*

Revised and Expanded

D0723530

THE INSTITUTE OF JESUIT SOURCES

Saint Louis

No. 23 in Series IV: Studies in Jesuit Topics

In its original form, this work appeared in *Studies in the Spirituality of Jesuits* 25, no. 2 (March 1993).

The Institute of Jesuit Sources
3601 Lindell Boulevard
St. Louis, MO 63108
        tel: [314] 977-7257
      fax: [314] 977-7263
e-mail: IJS@SLU.edu

Library of Congress Catalogue Card Number 00-103356
ISBN 1-880810-39-5

CONTENTS

John R. Donahue, S.J., is professor of Biblical Studies at the Jesuit School of Theology and at the Graduate Theological Union, Berkeley, Cal. He previously taught at the Divinity School of Vanderbilt University and more recently at the University of Notre Dame. He is the author of *Are You the Christ? The Trial of Jesus in the Gospel of Mark* (1973), *The Theology and Setting of Discipleship in the Gospel of Mark* (1983), and *The Gospel in Parable: Metaphor, Narrative and Theology in the Synoptic Gospels* (1988). His interest in relating biblical studies to issues of social justice goes back to the essay "Biblical Perspectives on Justice" in *The Faith That Does Justice* (1977). He served as a consultant (1983–86) on biblical issues to the committee of the United States bishops that drafted the pastoral letter *Economic Justice for All* (1986). Fr. Donahue's address is Jesuit School of Theology at Berkeley, 1735 LeRoy Avenue, Berkeley, CA 94709–1193.

What Does the Lord Require?

A Bibliographical Essay on the Bible and Social Justice

INTRODUCTION TO THE REVISED EDITION

Over the last century the Catholic Church has responded to the changing social and economic challenges of the modern world with a wide variety of official teaching, beginning with the encyclical letter of Pope Leo XIII *On the Condition of Labor* (*Rerum novarum*, 1891). This teaching has intensified since the landmark encyclical of Pope John XXIII *Christianity and Social Progress* (*Mater et magistra*, 1961), which was soon followed by *Peace on Earth* (*Pacem in terris*, 1963) and the major document of Vatican II, *The Pastoral Constitution on the Church in the Modern World* (*Gaudium et spes*, Dec. 7, 1965). Soon an important encyclical of Pope Paul VI appeared, *The Development of Peoples* (*Populorum progressio*, 1967) and the apostolic letter *A Call to Action* (*Octogesima adveniens*, 1971), which themselves were followed by the statement of the synod of bishops entitled "Justice in the World" (Nov. 30, 1971), with its oft quoted and still debated statement that "action on behalf of justice and participation in the transformation of the world fully appear to us as a constitutive dimension of the preaching of the Gospel." Pope John Paul II issued three major encyclicals dealing directly with questions of social and economic justice: *On Human Work* (*Laborem exercens*, 1981), *On Social Concerns* (*Sollicitudo rei socialis*, 1987), and *On the Hundredth Anniversary* (*Centesimus annus*, 1991). In the exhortations delivered while visiting particular locales, this pope has also focused on issues of social justice, freedom, and concern for the disparity between wealthy and poor nations .

In the United States, beginning with the famous "Program of Social Reconstruction" (1919) and a subsequent pastoral letter, the

1

bishops of the United States, initially under the leadership of Rev. John A. Ryan, addressed a wide variety of social concerns, culminating in their two major statements during the 1980s, *The Challenge of Peace: God's Promise and Our Response* (1983) and *Economic Justice for All: Pastoral Letter on Catholic Social Teaching and the U.S. Economy* (1986). Elsewhere in North America, the Canadian bishops also issued significant statements on social justice, especially *Ethical Reflections on the Economic Crisis* (January 1983; regarding this, see Baum, *Ethics and Economics*, below, p. 8). Especially important were the two general conferences of Latin American Bishops at Medellín in 1968 and Puebla in 1979. Likewise, major non-Catholic bodies, such as the World Council of Churches and local church organizations, showed strong leadership on issues of justice and peace.

Papal teaching, statements by groups of local bishops, and a rich body of theological reflection, while conditioned by time and circumstances, have yielded a rich trove of concerns and principles conducive to a just and humane society. At the risk of oversimplification, I will enumerate some of these: the essential link between the social and religious dimensions of life; the dignity of the human person, who possesses fundamental rights that are independent of sex, age, nationality, ethnic origin, religion, or economic status; the extension of the understanding of rights to include economic rights; promotion of the common good or, rather, the good of the community, with a realization that the needs of the marginal take precedence over the privileges of the prosperous; a deep concern for the poor and all those who are marginalized or adversely affected in a given economic situation ("the preferential option for the poor"); the common ownership of the goods of the earth and the summons to stewardship of the world's resources; and finally, a sense of global solidarity (especially in the social teaching of Pope John Paul II).

The same period that witnessed the rise of Catholic social teaching was also the century of the biblical renewal within Catholicism. Yet the social teaching was based almost exclusively on the Catholic natural-law tradition mediated primarily through Scholastic philosophy and theology. Though the two great streams of renewal flowed side by side rather than together, certain movements within them began to link the concerns of Catholic social teaching with biblical reflection.

The biblical renewal had its most significant impact on the development of liberation theology (see Hennelly, below, p. 9). The Bible provided a rich storehouse of motifs and texts that enabled people to reflect on their lives in light of revelation, while challenging previously held positions. Not surprisingly, the exodus, or the liberation of an oppressed people from Egypt, became a prime symbol that spoke to people suffering contemporary forms of oppression. In the seminal work of Gustavo Gutiérrez, "liberation" has a threefold meaning: "political liberation, human liberation throughout history, and admission to communion with God" (see *A Theology of Liberation*, 103, on p. 9 below). Despite the inaccurate criticism that liberation theology secularizes salvation and glosses over things like sin and forgiveness, Gutiérrez sees these three forms of liberation as integrally related.

Liberation theology also drew on the Hebrew Bible for other major themes, such as the prophetic attack on unbridled power and wealth, and the defense of the poor and oppressed, which developed into the somewhat controversial articulation of "the preferential option for the poor." When liberation theologians turned to the New Testament, the role of the historical Jesus in proclaiming and enacting the reign of God became crucial (see Bussmann and Batstone, below, p. 9). Liberation theology stood against the dominant trends of much European scholarship that viewed Jesus as an apocalyptic preacher little interested in this world. Very much influenced by the Lukan picture of Jesus, liberation theologians presented a prophetic Jesus who took the side of the marginal and the poor and entered into conflict with oppressive power. Shortly after the murder of the Jesuits and laywomen in San Salvador in November 1989, Jon Sobrino, who, of all the liberation theologians, has presented the most sophisticated and sustained studies of Jesus, wrote:

> The term "liberation theology" is a slogan and I don't care about slogans, but for Latin America I believe it is the most adequate theology. To live the Christian faith today is to do what Jesus of Nazareth did 20 centuries ago. If we share his views on wealth and poverty, on power and humility, on denouncing sin and telling the truth, then we can be called liberation theologians. If we are ready to share his destiny of being slandered and persecuted, if we are ready to show the great love—even by being put on the cross—then, yes, that is liberation theology.[1]

Crucial to the hermeneutics of liberation theology is an analysis of the human experience and social location *of those who read the Bible*. This involves a dialogue between the biblical text and the experiences of readers, factors that are often related by a process of analogy. This process of analogy is itself justified by the theological perspective that God continually acts in human history in ways which are disclosed primarily in the Bible, but which persist throughout human history.

---

[1] Quoted from Jon Sobrino, as recorded in the *San Jose Mercury*, Saturday, Nov. 25, 1989.

Though both official Church teaching and biblical scholars have leveled sustained criticisms against liberation theology, it has succeeded in moving beyond its original point of origin in Latin America. Even a cursory survey of current literature discloses a great number of works from Asia and Africa. Even though it was nurtured by Catholic theologians, liberation theology has also become the most ecumenical of theological disciplines, with contributions by liberal and evangelical Protestant scholars as well as by significant Jewish scholars. Feminist theology, which shares the same fundamental perspectives as does liberation theology, continues to be one of the most vital theological movements in the contemporary churches.

The writings of Pope John Paul II have drawn on biblical themes more than did previous papal statements. In *Laborem exercens* he speaks of human dignity and human destiny in the first two chapters of Genesis and comments, "An analysis of these texts makes us aware that they express—sometimes in an archaic way of manifesting thought—the fundamental truths about humanity." John Paul's most sustained use of the Bible occurs in his encyclical "On Social Concerns" *(Sollicitudo rei socialis)*, written to commemorate Pope Paul VI's *Populorum progressio*. Again the Pope turns to Gen. 1 and 2 to emphasize that men and women are created in the image of God; he goes on to note that

> [t]he story of the human race described by Sacred Scripture is, even after the fall into sin, a story of constant achievements which, although always called into question and threatened by sin, are nonetheless repeated, increased and extended in response to the divine vocation given from the beginning to man and woman (Gen. 1:26–28) and inscribed in the image they received.

The Parable of the Rich Man and Lazarus (Luke 16:19–31) is perhaps one of the texts most often cited in modern magisterial social teaching. It was used by Pope John XXIII in *Mater et magistra* (AAS 53 [1961]: 416ff.) and in *Pacem in terris* (AAS 55 [1963]: 289ff.). In *Gaudium et spes* the parable is cited to show that "everyone must consider his [or her] neighbor without exception as another self," to avoid imitating the rich man who had no concern for the poor Lazarus. In *Populorum progressio* (no. 47) Pope Paul VI expressed a hope for "a world where freedom is not an empty word, and where the poor man Lazarus can sit down at the same table with the rich man." In his world travels, Pope John Paul II frequently uses the parable, most notably in his address in Yankee Stadium on Oct. 2, 1979, where he observed that the rich man was condemned because "he failed to take notice" of Lazarus who sat at his door. The Pope states that this parable "must always be in our memory" and "form our conscience"; he declares that Christ demands openness "from the rich, the affluent, the economically advantaged [manifested] to the poor, the underdeveloped and the disadvantaged," and sees this as both an individual and national challenge (*Justice in the Marketplace*, p. 351). The key phrases in the papal statement are "always be in our memory" and "form our conscience." The biblical material does not give direct precepts, but necessarily influences and informs the Christian imagination and moral dispositions. Pope John Paul returned to this parable in *Sollicitudo rei socialis* (1987), stating, "It is essential to recognize each person's equal right to be seated at the common banquet instead of lying outside the door like Lazarus." Though this interpretation of the parable verges on the allegorical, I would argue that intertextually this is a legitimate way of making use of it and, further, that such an interpretation touches modern-day human imagination in a way that can evoke a response to the parable analogous to what was expected of Luke's original readers.

In *Centesimus annus* the Pope makes sparing use of Scripture, invoking again Genesis to undergird human dignity and the destination of the goods of the earth for common use. He also cites Matt. 25 and the Parable of the Good Samaritan to stress that everyone is responsible for the well-being of his or her brother or sister (no. 51). Still more important than that the Pope cites specific texts is that he sees the whole Christian tradition as affirming "the option or love of preference for the poor" (no. 42). Moreover, he declares that it is because of "her *evangelical duty* [emphasis mine] that she feels called to take her stand beside the poor, to discern the justice of their requests" (no. 39).

The most sustained use of the Bible in any Church document on social justice is found in the 1986 pastoral letter of the United States bishops entitled "Economic Justice for All." Here the bishops, recognizing the difficulty of bringing the Bible to bear on complex economic and social issues, call attention to "the Bible's deeper vision of God, of the purpose of creation, and of the dignity of human life in society." While offering no sustained biblical argument, the bishops selected five themes from the Bible that they judged especially pertinent to social issues today: (1) creation of all men and women in God's image, which stamps them with an inalienable dignity; (2) God's formation of a covenant community that is to live in justice and mutual concern; (3) the proclamation of God's reign by Jesus; (4) Jesus' formation of a community of disciples (5) that is to signalize itself by its special concern for the poor and marginal and (6) thus bequeath to history a legacy of hope and courage even amid failure and suffering. Despite the cursory and selective nature of the biblical treatment and the criticism in some circles that the use of the Bible by the bishops softens the prophetic critique of injustice, the themes selected provide a foundation for further theological reflection.

The concerns articulated in papal teaching, by local bishops' conferences, and by theologians and those engaged in direct ministry to victims of social and economic discrimination impacted major religious congregations, especially the Society of Jesus. Its Thirty-Second General Congregation (Dec. 2, 1974–March 7, 1975) bequeathed many challenges to contemporary Jesuits. Not the least of these was how to respond to the definition of our mission today as "the service of faith and the promotion of justice." This challenge came on the heels of the challenge issued by Vatican II to make Scripture the "soul of theology" (*Verbum Dei*, 24; *Optatam totius*, 16) and to nurture people from the table of both the word of God and the body of Christ (*Dei Verbum*, 21). In restoring the centrality of the ministry of the Word to faith and practice, the council also laid the mantle of conciliar authority on the biblical renewal that had maintained a rather tenuous toehold in the Church since *Divino afflante Spiritu* (Sept. 30, 1943).

For the last quarter century, Jesuits have been faced with the challenge to experience a conversion of heart, to relate their service of faith to the promotion of justice, and to embrace the intellectual task of finding resources for this in the Bible. Though this charge often seems daunting, in recent decades there have been a great number of studies by biblical scholars that offer fine resources for the theology and practice of the faith that does justice. I would like to survey and summarize some of the major issues and offer a selective bibliography for further study and use in different ministries. I make no attempt to be exhaustive and will for the most part mention titles available in English. While books and monographs will receive prime attention, I will also list important journal articles that might be of special help for personal study and teaching. At times it is difficult to say under which particular category a book should be listed, so frequent cross-referencing will be necessary.

General Congregation 34,[2] which met in Rome from January 5 to March 22, 1995, and was preceded by four years of preparation, in addition to updating the law of the Society in the area of "the faith that does justice," simultaneously confirmed the justice orientation of previous congregations, provided further theological foundation for this orientation and extended it into new areas such as justice and culture, interreligious dialogue, women in the Church, and cooperation with

---

[2] Hereafter abbreviated GC 34; other general congregations of the Society will be similarly abbreviated, for example, GC 32.

non-Jesuits in our ministries. It is clear that the very term "justice" is extended beyond its technical definitions and is used to evoke many different kinds of engagement that manifest concern with God's "making right" human life, and with right relationships in church and society. At the same time, there have been significant new publications in biblical studies since the first edition of this bibliography as well as new directions in theology. These will be treated in an additional section of the bibliograpy ("Contextual Theology and More Recent Developments in Biblical Studies").

In an overview of this kind, it would be tempting to begin with a discussion of the problem of hermeneutics—or **how** the biblical material can be used for theology and social ethics. Yet such a path can also lead to a labyrinth with no apparent sense of direction or exit. Even though exegesis can never be divorced from interpretation, I prefer to present descriptive studies first—**what** the Bible says—and then to offer some tentative guidelines on the interpretation and use of the biblical material.

This bibliography is partly in response to requests received over the years from Jesuits in different ministries who are responding generously to the call of GCs 32, 33, and 34, as well as from others—members of religious congregations, clerics, and laypeople. Some people want a few references for personal use; others want a longer list when preparing classes or retreats. Jesuits preparing for sabbaticals have asked for bibliographies. I have perhaps erred on the side of expansion, with the result that the number of works listed may seem daunting. Therefore, I have marked with an asterisk (*) those works I feel are most helpful and most readable. (They might also be worthy additions to a house library.) Works that are additions to this edition of the bibliography are marked with a plus sign (+). I have listed a large number of articles in periodicals, most of which would be accessible in any college or university library and would prove useful for those preparing courses or studying a topic in some depth.

▶   〰〰   ◀

Bibliography for the Introduction

Official Documents

A fine resource for official documents is United States Catholic Conference (USCC); Publishing Services; 3211 Fourth St. NE; Washington, D.C. 20017-1194; tele.: 800-235-8722.

Baum, Gregory, and Duncan Cameron. *Ethics and Economics: Canada's Catholic Bishops on the Economic Crisis.* Toronto: James Lorimer, Publ. 1984. A statement of the Canadian bishops, "Ethical Reflection on the Economic Crisis," with extended commentary.

Byers, David M., ed. *Justice in the Marketplace: Collected Statements of the Vatican and the U.S. Catholic Bishops on Economic Policy, 1891–1984.* Washington, D.C.: National Conference of Catholic Bishops (NCCB), 1985). A comprehensive collection of documents.

The Church in the Present-Day Transformation of Latin America. Washington, D.C.: USCC, 1977. Translation of final texts of Medellín Conference.

Eagleson, J., and P. Scharper, eds. *Puebla and Beyond.* Maryknoll, N.Y.: Orbis, 1980. Translation of the final document.

Economic Justice for All: Pastoral Letter on Catholic Social Teaching and the U.S. Economy. Issued by the National Conference of Catholic Bishops, Nov. 18, 1986. Adapts traditional Catholic Social teaching to United States context. See also *Tenth Anniversary Edition of Economic Justice for All,* which includes "A Catholic Framework for Economic Life," comprising ten points in both Spanish and English to summarize fundamental perspectives and facilitate discussion.

Gremillion, Joseph, ed. *The Gospel of Peace and Justice*: Catholic Social Teaching since Pope John. Maryknoll: Orbis, 1976.

John Paul II, Pope. *Sollicitudo rei socialis (On Social Concern).* Encyclical letter, Dec. 30, 1987. Available from NCCB.

———. *Centesimus annus (On the Hundredth Anniversary of* Rerum Novarum*).* Encyclical letter, May 1, 1992.

Mainelli, Vincent P., ed. *Official Catholic Teachings: Social Justice.* Wilmington, N.C.: McGrath Publ. Co, 1978. A collection of official documents from "Mater et magistra" to 1976.

O'Brien, David J., and Thomas A. Shannon, eds. *Catholic Social Thought: The Documentary Heritage.* Maryknoll, N.Y.: Orbis, 1992. This is the most up to date collection of documents and contains good introductions and brief commentaries. The older collections (Gremillion, Byers) remain helpful, since they often cover statements not found elsewhere, along with important introductions and comments.

Discussions and Surveys of Catholic Social Teaching

Coleman, John A., S.J., ed. *One Hundred Years of Catholic Social Thought: Celebration and Challenge.* Maryknoll, N.Y.: Orbis, 1991. Especially helpful are David J. O'Brien, "A Century of Catholic Social Teaching: Contexts and Comments"; John A. Coleman, "Neither Liberal nor Socialist: The Originality of Catholic Social Teaching," Archbp. Rembert G. Weakland, O.S.B, "The Economic Pastoral Letter Revisited."

Curran, Charles E. *American Catholic Social Ethics: Twentieth Century Approaches.* Notre Dame: University of Notre Dame Press, 1982. Excellent survey focusing on individuals and movements.

Curran, Charles E., and Richard A. McCormick, eds. *Official Catholic Social Teaching.* Readings in Moral Theology, no. 5. New York, N.Y.: Paulist Press, 1986.

Dwyer, Judith, ed. *The New Dictionary of Catholic Social Thought.* Collegeville, Minn.: Liturgical Press, 1994.

Massaro, Thomas. *Living Justice: Catholic Social Teaching in Action.* Franklin, Wisc.: Sheed & Ward, 2000. Integration of Scripture and Church teaching with suggestions for application.

Schuck, Michael Joseph. *That They Be One: The Social Teaching of the Papal Encyclicals, 1740–1989.* Washington, D.C.: Georgetown University Press, 1991.

Schultheis, Michael J., Edward P. De Berri, and Peter Henriot. *Our Best Kept Secret: The Rich Heritage of Catholic Social Teaching.* Washington, D.C.: Center of Concern, 1987. An outline of major documents with discussion questions.

Liberation Theology

The bibliography on this area is so vast that here we stress only bibliographical resources, surveys, and representative works.

Batstone, David. *From Conquest to Struggle: Jesus of Nazareth in Latin America.* Albany, N.Y.: State University of New York Press, 1991.

Bussmann, Claus. *Who Do You Say? Jesus Christ in Latin American Liberation Theology.* Maryknoll, N.Y.: Orbis, 1985. A good survey of different understandings of Jesus that have emerged.

Comblin, Joseph. *Called for Freedom: The Changing Context of Liberation Theology.* Maryknoll, N.Y.: Orbis, 1998. A powerful assessment of the achievements and problems of liberation theology by one its leading exponents.

Ellacuría, Ignacio, and Jon Sobrino, eds. *Mysterium Liberationis: Fundamental Concepts of Liberation Theology.* Maryknoll, N.Y.: Orbis, 1993.

Gutiérrez, Gustavo. *A Theology of Liberation: 15th Anniversary Edition with a New Introduction by the Author.* Maryknoll, N.Y.: Orbis, 1988. When first published in Spanish in 1971, it quickly became a landmark work for liberation theology and appropriation of biblical themes.

Haight, Roger. *An Alternative Vision: An Interpretation of Liberation Theology.* New York: Paulist Press, 1985. A good overview of liberation theology's impact of on theology.

Hennelly, Alfred T. *Liberation Theology: A Documentary History.* Maryknoll, N.Y.: Orbis, 1990.

McGovern, Arthur F. *Liberation Theology and Its Critics: Toward an Assessment.* Maryknoll: Orbis, 1989.

Musto, Ronald G. *Liberation Theologies: A Research Guide.* New York: Garland Pub., 1991.

Rowland, Christopher, ed. *The Cambridge Companion to Liberation Theology.* Cambridge/New York: Cambridge University Press, 1999.

Sobrino, Jon. *Christology at the Crossroads: A Latin American Approach.* Maryknoll, N.Y.: Orbis, 1978.

_____. *Jesus the Liberator: A Historical-Theological Reading of Jesus of Nazareth.* Maryknoll, N.Y.: Orbis, 1993.

General Studies of Biblical Ethics

Concern for the faith that does justice demands reflection on both the theological meaning of biblical texts and their ethical implication. This would logically demand reflection on the Bible's understanding of God (theology), of the human condition (anthropology), of the manner in which men and women are freed from sin and death and restored to intimacy with God (soteriology), and of the proper relation to God and fellow humans (ethics). The works I list below, while concentrating on ethics, are a rich source of biblical theology.

▶ ◀

Bibliography on General Studies of Biblical Ethics

Though I will list bibliography for each topic, I cannot recommend strongly enough the *New Jerome Biblical Commentary.* It represents the most up-to-date biblical scholarship and contains excellent bibliographies. Highly recommended on particular topics is the recently published *Anchor Bible Dictionary,* ed. David N. Freedman, 6 vols. (New York: Bantam Doubleday, 1992). Also furnishing brief treatments of important topics are the *Harper's Bible Dictionary,* ed. Paul Achtemier (San Francisco: Harper and Row, 1985), and +Carroll Stuhlmueller, ed., *The Collegeville Pastoral Dictionary of Biblical Theology* (Collegeville, Minn.: The Liturgical Press, 1996). Recommended are the articles "Justice," "Poor," and "Prophet/prophecy."

*Birch, Bruce C. *What Does the Lord Require? The Old Testament Call to Social Witness.* Philadelphia: Westminster Press, 1985. More popular presentations of material which Birch later develops in *Let Justice Roll.*

———. *Let Justice Roll: The Old Testament, Ethics and the Christian Life.* Louisville, Ky.: Westminster/John Knox Press, 1991. The fruit of over twenty years of reflection, often in dialogue with Larry Rasmussen (an ethicist), this is the best available survey of OT ethics, with great sensitivity to social issues. It surveys the literature in a canonical and historical order from Genesis through the wisdom literature.

Birch, Bruce C., and Larry L. Rasmussen. *The Predicament of the Prosperous.* Philadelphia: Westminster Press, 1978. This work arose from discussions in both academic and pastoral settings. The first part treats of the challenges and dilemmas facing "the predominantly white, prosperous, middle-class churches of the United States" (13),[3] while the second part offers reflections on biblical themes and motifs that challenge such an audience. It is a model of interdisciplinary work and presents a fine method for dialogue with biblical texts.

+Ceresko, Anthony B. *Introduction to the Old Testament: A Liberation Perspective.* Maryknoll, N.Y.: Orbis, 1992. Ceresko is professor of Old Testament at St. Peter's Pontifical Institute in Bangalore, India.

+Felder, Cain H. "Toward a New Testament Hermeneutic for Justice," a Howard University Lecture, *Journal of Religious Thought* 45 (1988:) 10–28. An interesting study by a leading African-American theologian.

*Haughey, John C., ed. *The Faith That Does Justice.* New York/Ramsey: Paulist Press, 1977. Though a bit dated, the essays by Donahue, "Biblical Perspectives on Justice," and Haughey, "Jesus as the Justice of God," offer a good introduction to important biblical themes and texts.

Mott, Stephen C. *Biblical Ethics and Social Change.* New York: Oxford University Press, 1982. Organized thematically with coverage of both testaments. Mott represents a group of evangelical scholars committed to issues of social justice. Part 1: "A Biblical Theology of Social Involvement"; Part 2: "Paths to Justice." He views the Church as a "counter cultural" community dedicated to nonviolent implementation of social change.

Ogletree, Thomas W. *The Use of the Bible in Christian Ethics: A Constructive Essay.* Philadelphia: Fortress Press, 1983. A sophisticated attempt by an ethicist to bridge the gap between biblical studies and ethics. The chapter on "covenant and commandment" (47–85) is one of the best treatments of the implications of covenant for a theology of social justice. This book also treats the Synoptic portrayals of eschatological existence and Paul's gospel of freedom.

THE OLD TESTAMENT

Studies of Old Testament Themes and Blocks of Literature

While the biblical literature evolved over the centuries from diverse oral traditions to blocks of literature, its canonical shape was fixed rather late. For example, Gen. 1–12 (creation and primeval history), though it treated "at the beginning," was appended to the national history (Exodus through Deuteronomy) only after the exile (586–536 B.C.); and the *Torah* receives its final shape only between 300 and 200 B.C.

While qualified by subsequent scholarship, the positions of Von Rad and Noth still offer an excellent way to survey the OT. Von Rad

---

[3] Unless otherwise indicated, numbers enclosed in parentheses, as in this instance, refer to the page(s) of the book or article to which reference is made.

argued that the Pentateuchal traditions developed from credal formulas such as Deut. 6:20–25, 26:1–12, and Josh. 24:2–13, which provided the fundamental themes of Israel's faith, where a "theme" is understood as a basic act of God by which the people are constituted. When expanded into a narrative, these themes attract related themes and motifs. Noth underlined five such themes: *(a)* the guidance out of Egypt (Exodus), *(b)* the "guidance into arable land" (Joshua), *(c)* the promise to the patriarchs (Gen. 12–50), *(d)* the guidance (and testing) in the wilderness, and *(e)* the revelation at Sinai. I will offer some reflection and bibliography on two of these themes (Exodus and Covenant); but I will begin with the creation story, which is an important "overture" to the salvation history of Genesis through Joshua.

The final "canonical" shaping of the Pentateuch is important theologically. At its center stands the covenant of Sinai, which forms those liberated from Egypt into a nation with responsibilities and duties. God's *gift* of liberation involves a *demand* for fidelity. The older story of the taking of the land, with its triumphalistic tendencies, has been supplanted by the beginning of the Deuteronomic history (Deuteronomy), with its theme of recurring infidelity.

Bibliography on Old Testament Themes

+Laffey, Alice. *The Pentateuch: A Liberation-Criticial Reading.* Minneapolis, Minn.: Fortress, 1998.

Noth, Martin. "The Major Themes of the Tradition in the Pentateuch and Their Origin." In *A History of the Pentateuchal Traditions,* trans. B. Anderson, 46–62. Englewood Cliffs, N.J.: Prentice Hall, 1972.

Von Rad, Gerhard. *The Problem of the Hexateuch and Other Essays.* New York: McGraw Hill, 1966. A landmark study on the development of the Pentateuch.

Sanders, James A. *Torah and Canon.* Philadelphia: Fortress Press, 1972. An interesting discussion of the formation of the OT.

Creation (Gen. 1–11)

A generation of Jesuits was nurtured on two perspectives that are no longer helpful for understanding creation in the Bible. The first was that Gen. 1–3 (culminating in the fall and the expulsion of Adam and Eve) could be read as an independent block of material. This was undergirded by the use of these chapters primarily for the doctrine of original sin. The second was that the biblical creation narratives dealt with cosmology. This latter view was supported by debates over evolution. As Claus Westermann has strongly argued, the whole primeval history (Gen. 1–11) must be read as a unity, culminating in the Tower of Babel. Theologically, creation is not concerned with the origin of the world and the universe, but rather with the situation in which later readers found themselves. Technically, these narratives are "etiological": they describe the causes of the yearning for God, the gap between God and humanity, and the divisions within humanity itself.

Today scholars often reject the division of the Pentateuch into four clearly defined literary "sources" (J, E, P, D), and speak instead of blocks of tradition that are often less separable than the reconstructions of the older "documentary hypothesis." Still, it is customary to see two major perspectives in the creation account. The "preamble" or first account (1:1–2:4a) is attributed to the priestly tradition (P) and is the later of the two accounts. The second account, which narrates the creation of the man and the woman, their offspring, and the spread of civilization (2:4b–4:26), is attributed to J (the Yahwist).

Contemporary reflection on social justice often turns to these accounts to ground human dignity in the creation in God's image, to argue for the common claim of all humanity to the world's resources and, more frequently now, for reflection on ecological issues. I will now simply indicate elements in the text that are important.

The first account describes a primitive cosmology in rhythmic cadences marked off by a division into "days," with the frequent refrain that "it was good" (Gen. 1:4, 10, 12, 18, 21, 25), culminating in the final day when God views all creation as "very good" (v. 31). Claus Westermann, whose extensive writings on creation are the best resource for a proper biblical theology of creation, notes that these narratives reveal the priestly stress that all events have their origin in God's commanding word. They prepare for the revelation on Sinai, when God's word forms the somewhat chaotic throng into a people (*Creation*, 42). He also notes that by placing the separation of night and day through the creation of "light" before the creation of "space," the author stresses that human life is temporal and historical.

The goodness of creation is not something that men and women affirm but is a divine proclamation. By locating the creation story as a preamble to the whole sacred history, the priestly writer proclaims the goodness of all creation, even though the narrative that unfolds depicts the catastrophic results of sin on both nature and human history (Westermann, *Genesis*, 60–64). The proper response to creation is praise and thanksgiving even amid suffering and catastrophe, since God has affirmed that nature and its power are "good." Two obvious implications arise from Genesis 1:1–2:4a: first, the response to creation is reverence and praise, not exploitation, and second, humanity shares a solidarity with both the inanimate and animate world in owing its existence to the word of God.

The creation narrative of P reaches its summit in Gen. 1:26: "Let us make humankind in our image, according to our likeness and let them have dominion. . . ." This is then followed by the blessing of man and woman, the command to be fruitful and multiply, and God's resting on the seventh day. Man and woman created in the image of God is one of the most frequently cited texts to undergird human dignity and human rights. Created "in the image of God" in its original context does not mean some human quality (intellect or free will) or the possession of "sanctifying grace." Two interpretations enjoy some exegetical support today. One view is that, just as ancient Near Eastern kings erected "images" of themselves in subject territory, so humans are God's representatives, to be given the same honor due God. Claus Westermann argues that the phrase means that humans were created to be God's counterpart, creatures analogous to God with whom God can speak and who will hear God's word (Genesis: A Practical Commentary, 10). In either of these interpretations, all men and women prior to identification by race, social status, religion, or sex are worthy of respect and reverence.

The term "have dominion" (see "to till and to keep" [Gen. 2:15]) has often been criticized by ecologists as the warrant for a utilitarian view of creation or as justification for the exploitation of creation for human convenience. The Hebrew term is used in other places to describe the royal care that characterizes a king as God's vice-regent (Pss. 72:8, 110:2; see also Ps. 8:5–9). Like ancient kings, men and women are to be the mediators of prosperity and well-being (Westermann, Genesis, 51–53). In neither creation account is the human being given "dominion" over another human being. This is not part of the human constitution. Reverential care for God's creation rather than exploitation is the mandate given humanity in this section of Genesis.

The second and older creation story (2:4b–3:24) is more anthropomorphic and more dramatic. It may be composed of two originally different stories. One deals with the creation of "man" (Heb. 'iš) from the clay of the earth, yet notices that this creature was incomplete without a complementary partner ('iššâ). The other, as Westermann stresses, is the spread of sin running through Gen. 1–11 (see also 4:1–6; 6:1–4, 6–9; 11:1–10). This latter motif has dominated the history of exegesis of the creation account.

Two elements of the creation of "man" and "woman" are important for contemporary reflection. First, as a story of mythic beginnings (akin to other ancient myths of "androgyny"), the narrative stresses the complementarity of male and female. The "human" is male and female united as "one flesh" (2:24), not understood simply as a description of marriage, but as a basic fact of prototypical human existence. On the anthropological level, this calls for a recognition of the presence of "male" and "female" in every human. On the social level, it means that the human condition can never be defined or named in terms of the dominant characteristics or activity of one sex.

Proper understanding of the "fall," or sin of the first parents, also has implications for a theological grounding of social justice. Taking this narrative on its own terms requires a bracketing of its Pauline and post-Pauline interpretation (Rom. 5:12–20, 2 Cor. 11:3, 1 Tim. 2:13–15), as well as of the Augustinian doctrine of "original sin." The narrative remains, however, a rich source for understanding human evil and alienation from God.

It explains the human potentiality for evil, no matter how gifted one may be. The human person according to Gen. 2:4b–3:24 is created for life and knowledge. The ultimate test or temptation in this narrative is to "be like God" (3:5), knowing good and evil, which is "knowledge in a wide sense, inasmuch as it relates to the mastery of human existence" (Westermann, *Creation*, 92f.). The temptation is always to an autonomy that seeks this apart from the limits of being human or from life in community. Sin is overstepping the limits of the human condition by aspiring to divine power. It can take place through action (the woman) or through complicity (the man). Their desire to be like God sadly separates them from God.

After the "fall" the narrative relates the trial and the punishment (3:8–24). The expected punishment of 3:3 ("you shall die") does not occur. Instead, the harmony of their earlier status is destroyed. Desire for human autonomy leads to alienation and breakdown of community with nature and between man and woman. It is important to note that the subordinate position of women (3:16f.), which reflects the de facto situation of women in ancient society, is not something that was to be part of the original blessing of creation, but arises from human sinfulness. Alienation between the earth and humans (3:17–19) is likewise a result of sin. While the "work" of cultivating and caring for the earth is intrinsic to the human condition prior to sin, "toil" is its consequence.

The narratives of Gen. 4–11 capture the ambivalence of the human condition. As civilization grows through the multiplication of occupations (farmers and shepherds) and through the invention of elements of culture (4:19–22), sin is depicted as "crouched at the door" (4:7), and humans continually overstep their limits. This culminates in the Tower of Babel, where humans attempt to invade the realm of God. Though a reprise of the attempt to be like gods, the narrative has political ramifications. Though set in "primeval time," it receives its final form after the Babylonian exile. The fate of Babylon, with its pretensions of world rule and its idolatrous self-exaltation, only to be split apart by the onslaught of Cyrus, is reflected in the Tower of Babel. The spread of sin culminates in the idolatrous pretensions of national power.

These chapters of Genesis are also important for reflection on the somewhat controversial notion of "social sin." The term was first used by theologians and derived from reflection on certain official Church statements. While speaking of the economic, political, and social order, Vatican II, in its decree on the Church in the Modern World, declared that "the structure of human affairs is flawed by the consequences of sin" (*Gaudium et spes*, no. 25). The 1971 Synod of Bishops noted that the present-day situation of the world is marked by "the grave sin of injustice" (no. 29) and called for a renewal of heart "based on the recognition of sin in its individual and social manifestations" (no. 51). In their pastoral letter on racism, *Brothers and Sisters to Us* (Nov. 14, 1979), the U.S. bishops describe racism as social sin "in that each one of us in varying degrees, is responsible. All of us are in some measure accomplices" (*Origins* 9, no. 24 [Nov. 29, 1979]: 383–89). The 1986 letter of the United States bishops on the economy, *Economic Justice for All*, said that the elite's exclusion of masses of people in developing countries from use of their own natural resources is a form of social sin (no. 77). In 1972 and 1973 Peter Henriot, S.J., wrote two important articles that focused attention on the issue of social sin and did much to introduce the term into contemporary theology (see below). Social sin came to be identified with structures of injustice, discrimination, or oppression in which men and women participate either by acting directly or by being passive accomplices.

Though Vatican and papal statements have cautioned that sin is primarily a freely chosen act of an individual, they have allowed for the term in an analogous or extended sense. (See especially the *Apostolic Exhortation on Reconciliation and Penance*, issued on Dec. 11, 1984, by Pope John Paul II in response to the 1983 Synod of Bishops [*Origins* 14, no. 27 (Dec. 20, 1984): 434–58, especially pp. 441f.].) Actually, the biblical notion of sin is primarily social and only gradually becomes individual. In the Genesis accounts sin is a power that "lurks at the door" (4:7) and spreads through humanity. The prophets indict the sins of groups rather than of individuals, as in the denunciations of the nations or the indictments of "the house of Israel" (Amos 1:3–2:16). Those judged at the end of Matthew (25:31–46) for neglect of the little ones are "nations," not individuals. Paul conceives of sin as a power that threatens to rule over people's lives (Rom. 5:12–21); and, in the Gospel of John, Jesus is the lamb who will take away the "sin of the world" (1:29; *not* "sins," as in the Latin translation "qui tollis peccata mundi").

The primeval history of Gen. 1–11 thus provides a rich resource for reflection on issues crucial to faith and justice. Men and women are God's representatives and conversation partners in the world, with a fundamental dignity that must be respected and fostered. They are to exist in interdependence and mutual support and are to care for the world with respect, as for a gift received from God. Yet the human condition is flawed by a drive to overstep the limits of the human situation and to claim autonomous power. The result of this is violence (Cain and Abel) and idolatry (the Tower of Babel). The Genesis narrative functions both as a normative description of the human condition before God and a critical principle against any power that distorts or usurps the dignity of humanity or God's claim over men and women.

Bibliography on Genesis and on Social Sin

On Genesis

Anderson, Bernhard, ed. *Creation in the Old Testament.* Philadelphia: Fortress Press; London: S.P.C.K., 1984. A fine collection of classic and contemporary essays. See especially G. Landes, "Creation and Liberation," 135–51, and B. Anderson, "Creation and Ecology," 152–71.

Clifford, Richard J., S.J. "Creation in the Hebrew Bible." In *Physics, Philosophy and Theology,* ed. Robert Russell, William R. Stoeger, S.J., and George V. Coyne, S.J., 151–70. Vatican City State: Vatican Observatory, 1988 (available from University of Notre Dame Press). An excellent survey of biblical texts, with sensitivity to questions posed by modern science.

*Trible, Phyllis. *God and the Rhetoric of Sexuality.* Philadelphia: Fortress Press, 1978. By combining a "close reading" of the biblical text, rhetorical criticism, and feminist hermeneutics, Trible presents a major contribution to a proper reading of Gen. 1–3.

*Westermann, Claus. *Creation.* Philadelphia: Fortress Press, 1974. Westermann is an outstanding biblical theologian, and this short volume (123 pp.) is the best thing available on creation.

———. *Genesis 1–11: A Commentary.* Vol. 1. Minneapolis: Augsburg, 1984; vol. 2 (1985) covers Gen. 12–36, and vol. 3 (1986) treats Gen. 37–50. An invaluable reference commentary on Genesis. The commentaries in this series *(Biblischer Kommentar)* are notable for their coverage of subsequent theological interpretations of biblical passages, done with great ecumenical sensitivity.

———. *Genesis: A Practical Commentary.* Grand Rapids: Eerdmans, 1987. Along with *Creation,* this offers a fine digest of Westermann's exegesis.

———. *Genesis: An Introduction.* Minneapolis: Fortress Press, 1991. It contains the introductions to important sections taken from the three-volume commentary.

On Social Sin

Henriot, Peter. "The Concept of Social Sin." *Catholic Mind* 71 (Oct 1973): 38–53.

———. "Social Sin and Conversion: A Theology of the Church's Social Involvement." *Chicago Studies* 11 (Summer 1972): 115–30. Important seminal articles.

Kerans, Patrick. *Sinful Social Structures.* New York: Paulist, 1974.

O'Keefe, M. *What Are They Saying about Social Sin?* New York: Paulist, 1990. A helpful overview.

Exodus: The Leading Out from Egypt

The primeval history is followed by the patriarchal history (Gen. 12–50), which begins with God's call and covenant with Abraham and Sarah (Gen. 12:1–9, 15:1–21, 17:1–27); these constitute the foundation narrative for the emergence of Israel as a people. The subsequent stories of the children of Abraham describe how God's promise is maintained through adversity. Though these narratives are foundational, it is the narratives of Exodus and Sinai that constitute Israel's identity. I will offer some reflections on the Exodus and discuss covenant in the context of the Sinai covenant.

The Exodus from Egypt (Exod. 1:1–15:21) has emerged as one of the most dominant biblical events for a biblical theology of liberation from evil and unjust social structures. There are two dangers here: the first, that a too generalized statement of its meaning absolves people from close attention to the rich theological dimensions of the text; the second, that the exodus is considered in isolation from other biblical themes. While liberation from oppression is a fundamental aspect of the exodus narrative, it is not simply *freedom from* that is important, but *freedom for* the formation of a community that lives under the covenant. As Michael Walzer says, the journey of Israel is to a "bonded freedom."

Exodus and covenant, liberation and commitment must be taken together as part of one process.

The narrative falls roughly into the following divisions: *(a)* the oppression of the Hebrew people (1:1–2:22); *(b)* the preparation of Moses as the agent of liberation (2:23–7:7); *(c)* the plagues on Egypt, culminating in the death of Egypt's firstborn (7:8–13:16); and *(d)* the crossing of the sea, the destruction of the Egyptian armies, and the hymn of Miriam (13:17–15:21).

The description of Israel's bondage has become paradigmatic of oppression. In fulfillment of the promise to Abraham and through no action of their own, other than fulfilling God's command to be fruitful and multiply, the people grow numerous and become a threat to a dominant power. The initial response is one of massive forced labor. Maimonides (A.D. 1135–1204) described this as service without limits of time or purpose (Walzer, *Exodus,* 27). The second major threat, the killing of the male children, is in effect genocide. The people's identity will be slowly but surely destroyed. Theologically, it is a challenge to the fidelity of God manifest in the promises to Abraham.

Though it is customary to mark the beginning of the liberation from the birth of Moses (Exod. 2:1–20), the "revolt of the midwives" (1:15–22) is an important paradigm of resistance to oppression. It is described briefly: "But the midwives feared God; they did not do as the King of Egypt commanded them, but they let the boys live" (1:17). These women, the daughters of Eve, the mother of all the living, commissioned to bring forth life in the world, reject the murderous command of Pharaoh. They do this in light of a higher law ("fearing God" [1:17, 21]). Therefore "God dealt well with the midwives, and the people multiplied and became very strong." On the narrative level, they allow the promise to continue and also prepare for the rescue of Moses from death (2:1–10).

The process of liberation continues with the "liberation" of the liberator. The agent of liberation must suffer the same fate as that of the people (threat of death, life as an alien in an alien land [Exod. 2:15, 3:22]). At the same time, the liberator must be equipped to meet the threat (3:1–11) and be the agent of a higher power (4:10f.). Liberation is a power struggle—between humans and their oppressors, but more fundamentally between God and the powers opposed to God.

The theophany at the burning bush and the call of Moses proclaim that liberation is fundamentally an act of God. God's action begins in 2:24 ("God heard their groaning and remembered his covenant") and is detailed in 3:7–12, which is a virtual summary of the identity of Yahweh as the compassionate God who enters human history. Immediately after the revelation of the name, Yahweh says, "I have *observed* the misery of the people; I have *heard* their cry; indeed I *know* their sufferings; I have *come down to deliver them*" (3:7–12; see also, "[B]y the tender mercy [compassion] of our God, the dawn from on high will break upon us" [Luke 1:78]).

The liberation itself unfolds through the sequence of ten plagues, divided into three triads culminating in the killing of the Egyptian firstborn and the "passing over" of the firstborn of Israel. In the plagues nature itself turns against the Egyptians, almost in revulsion at their oppression of God's people. As the plagues escalate, the issue again becomes the nature of God and the usurpation of divine power. In 9:16–17a God speaks through Moses to Pharaoh: "This is why I let you live: to show you my power, and to make my name resound through all the earth. You are still exalting yourself against my people."

In the final plague, the Passover (11:1–13:16), the "P" source (12:1–38) becomes prominent, showing that the narrative had become "the cult legend" for the later celebration of Passover. Here the Exodus receives the character of *anamnesis,* something to be re-presented and celebrated annually. Thus it continues to shape the identity of the people and reveal the nature God.

I will offer a few observations on Exodus as a paradigm of liberation. Liberation is a power struggle in which the issues of oppression are progressively highlighted. Pharaoh begins with concern about the growth of an alien population, but his real concern is whether he will be their "god" or whether they will be free to worship the one who called their ancestors. Oppression and idolatry are never far apart. Liberation does not come from the most oppressed members of the community. Moses is nurtured at the center of Egypt's power and is equipped to enter its world. Through his own "conversion" and preparation by God, he becomes a prophet, one who speaks for God and for a people without a voice (see also, "[N]ever since has there arisen a prophet like Moses" [Deut. 34:10]). Yet, as I will note below, "liberation" is but one aspect of a true concept of freedom. Israel's journey is "from liberation to freedom," which is the ultimate theme of the wilderness wandering and the covenant at Sinai.

Bibliography on Exodus

Coats, George. *Moses: Heroic Man, Man of God.* Sheffield: Journal for the Study of the Old Testament Press, 1988. An academic study of the portrayal of Moses in the Hebrew Bible.

Croatto, J. Severino. *Exodus: A Hermeneutics of Freedom.* Maryknoll: Orbis, 1981. An important study of Exodus as the basis of a theology of liberation.

*Fretheim, Terence E. "Exodus." In *Interpretation: A Bible for Teaching and Preaching.* Louisville: John Knox, 1991. An excellent commentary, especially on Exod. 1–15, with sensitivity to issues of liberation and justice.

————. "The Plagues as Ecological Signs of Historical Disaster." *Journal of Biblical Literature* 110 (Fall 1991): 385–96. Fretheim argues that the plagues are signs that nature itself revolts against the moral injustice of Pharaoh's reign.

Pixley, George V. *Exodus: A Liberation Perspective.* Maryknoll: Orbis, 1987. A powerful but somewhat simplistic reading of the biblical text.

Walzer, Michael. *Exodus and Revolution.* New York: Basic Books, 1985. A very interesting study of the biblical text and the subsequent impact of the Exodus narrative, written by a political theorist (author of *Spheres of Justice*). +A strong criticism of Walzer has been presented by Edward W. Said, "Michael Walzer's 'Exodus and Revolution': A Canaanite Reading, *Grand Street* 5, no. 2 (Winter 1986): 86–106; with a reply by Walzer, *Grand Street* 5, no. 5 (Summer, 1986): 246–59

Wildavsky, Aaron. *The Nursing Father: Moses as a Political Leader.* University of Alabama Press, 1984. An interesting study by an eminent political scientist.

Wilderness Wandering and the Covenant at Sinai

In the sweep of salvation history, the people of Israel are on a journey to the land of promise from Exod. 13:17 through the books of Exodus, Leviticus, Numbers, and Deuteronomy, where Moses dies on Mt. Nebo gazing into a land he will not enter (Deut. 34:1–8). The long narrative thus becomes the context for interpreting how the liberated people are to live in community before God, and it constitutes the substance of the different law codes incorporated in this section. These represent traditions dating from the early nomadic origins of Israel to the latest postexilic redaction of the material. It is as if the American *Declaration of Independence,* the *Constitution,* its amendments, and the corpus of Supreme Court decisions were gathered into one book and all dated at the same time. Yet, in final canonical shape these Israelite codes are the *Torah,* the document that is the "constitution" of the people.

Of fundamental importance is the bracketing of the sojourn at Sinai (Exod. 19:1–Num. 10:10) by stories of the rebellions of the people in the wilderness. Examples would be Exod. 16f. (the gift of Manna and the water from the rock); Num. 11:16–34 (the revolt of the elders against Moses); and Num. 16:1–40 (the revolt of Dathan and Abiram). This is the root of the later ambivalence of "the wilderness" in Israel's traditions. It is the place of betrothal and first love (Sinai) and simultaneously the place of corporate disobedience.

The initial grumblings of the people center around a nostalgic remembrance of the "soft life" in Egypt, where slavery at least provided life's necessities (Exod. 15:24, 16:3, 17:3). The challenge they face at Sinai is to be transformed from a "liberated" people to a free, responsible people. Walzer, citing Rousseau, states that Moses' great achievement was to transform a herd of "wretched fugitives" who lacked virtue and courage into a "free people." They are challenged to adopt a way of life that is not freedom from regulation, but rather a "bondage in freedom," consisting of freely chosen obligations (Walzer, *Exodus and Revolution*, 53).

These initial soundings of the wilderness traditions are important for a proper liberation theology. Though beginning as a power struggle, liberation is a process rather than an event. Freedom from external oppression brings with it the challenge of mature appropriation of freedom through adoption of a way of life that, as we will see, does not reproduce the very evils which have been overthrown. As Norbert Lohfink states so cogently (see below), Israel is brought out of Egypt to form "a contrast society," not to reproduce the Egyptian mode of governance. For this reason principally I would argue that liberation cannot be the center or sole focus of biblical revelation. St. Paul will tell the Galatians, "[F]or freedom Christ has set us free" (Gal. 5:1), and then list a whole series of virtues that describe walking in the Spirit or living in freedom (Gal. 5:22–26). Too often the experience of oppression and the cry for liberation can produce a "moral holiday" for other virtues, during which the perceived oppressor is so demonized that, as Paolo Freire noted, those oppressed take on the attitudes of the oppressors. The sad current upheavals in the newly liberated nations of Eastern Europe show that liberation from an oppressive power is no guarantee of true freedom.

Covenant and Law

A covenant is basically "a formal agreement or treaty between two parties with each assuming some obligations" (Jeremiah Unterman, *Harper's Bible Dictionary*, 190). As is generally known, the Bible contains two major covenant forms. The first, modeled on the Hittite suzerainty treaty, contains a preamble, historical prologue, stated obligations, blessings, and often some stated symbol of ratification. Exod. 19–24 and Josh. 24 are influenced by this pattern. When broken, such covenants must be renewed. The second are "people of destiny" covenants, which cannot be broken and which express God's unaltered choice of an individual who will bear the destiny of the people (for instance, Gen. 17 [Abraham], 2 Sam. 7:1–17; see also Ps. 89:1–13 [the Davidic king]). The importance of covenant to considerations of justice is twofold: *(a)* in the covenant context Israel's distinctive understandings of law and justice emerge; and *(b)* the covenant reveals a God who wishes people to live in a community combining worship and obedience to him with care for neighbor, a God who remains faithful even when people break the covenant. Only in this context are conversion and change of heart a constant demand and possibility.

The Meaning of Justice

In my essay in *The Faith That Does Justice,* I attempted to describe the elusive biblical concept of *ṣĕdāqāh/ṣedeq* (with some allusion to its related concept of *mišpāṭ*). I stated there that *ṣĕdāqāh* is used for a wide variety of things. Some examples would be "God who has led me by the right way" (Gen. 24:48), "just" weights (Lev. 19:36), "You shall have honest balances, honest weights, an honest ephah (Deut. 25:15), "You shall have only a full and honest measure (see Ezek. 45:10), "just" sacrifices (Deut. 33:19; Pss. 4:5, 51:19). Scales are "just" when they give fair measure; paths are "just" when they get you where you should be going. "Justice" is also used in the sense of "victory" or saving act: "They repeat the triumphs (*ṣidqôth*) of the Lord" (Judg. 5:11) and "all the saving deeds of the Lord" (1 Sam. 12:7).

God is frequently characterized as "just" (2 Chron. 12:6; Neh. 9:8; Pss. 7:9, 103:17, 116:5; Isa. 30:18; Jer. 9:24), seeking and loving justice (Isa. 61:8; Pss. 11:7, 33:5, 37:38, 99:4); and justice is one of the stipulations of the covenant (Hos. 2:21, see below, and Jer. 9:23f.). The Bible speaks of a just individual who is in "right relation" to God and others, with a special concern for those "others" who are powerless or marginal (Job 4:3f., 29:12–16, 31:16–19; Prov. 31:9).

Justice conveys the sense of "rightness" or "integrity," things being as they should be. It is often associated with other concepts such as *šālōm* (peace), fidelity, and loving kindness.

Ps. 85:11: Kindness and truth shall meet *(ḥesed . . . ʾĕmet);*
justice and peace shall kiss *(ṣĕdāqāh . . . šālōm).*
Isa. 32:16: Right *(mišpāṭ)* will dwell in the desert
and justice *(ṣĕdāqāh)* in the orchard.
17: Justice will bring about peace;
right *(ṣĕdāqāh)* will produce calm and security.
Isa. 60:17: I will appoint peace your governor
and justice your ruler.

In Hos. 2:21 justice is one of the qualities of God's covenant with the people, which leads to proper knowledge of God.

I will espouse you to me forever;
I will espouse you in right and justice *(bĕ ṣedeq . . . bĕ mišpāṭ);*
in love *(bĕ ḥesed)* and in mercy *(bĕ raḥămîm)*
I will espouse you in fidelity (be ʾĕmūnāh)
and you shall know the Lord.

See also Jer. 22:15f., where the doing of justice is equated with knowledge of the Lord.

In 1977 I defined justice as "fidelity to the demands of a relationship." God is just when he acts as God should, defending or vindicating his people or punishing violations of the covenant. People are just when they are in right relationship to God and to other humans. My earlier reflections should be supplemented by the reflections of J. P. M. Walsh (*Mighty*, 1–12). Walsh underscores the social dimension of *ṣedeq* by describing it as "consensus" about what is right. People in all societies have some innate sense of this, even though it differs in concrete situations. Biblical revelation of *ṣedeq* involves the consensus that is to shape God's people. More carefully than I, Walsh relates *ṣedeq* to *mišpāṭ,* the implementation of justice *(ṣedeq)* by action (juridical or otherwise). Finally, he treats *nāqām* (literally, vengeance) as the process by which "consensus" or sense of rightness is restored. The thrust of Walsh's whole work is that the biblical tradition gives a different vision of these seminal concepts than does the modern liberal tradition. In the biblical traditions these terms define a consensus against the misuse of power and disclose a God who is on the side of the marginal.

In premonarchic Israel the responsibility for justice in the society was laid on the whole community. With the advent of the monarchy and under the influence of Ancient Near-Eastern royal ideology, the king, as God's vice-regent, enforces justice in the land and is the protector of the marginal. (See Ps. 89 for a virtual "job description" of the king, especially 89:14: "Righteousness and justice are the foundation of your throne"; see also Pss. 45:8; 72, especially vv. 3f.; 85:11, 99:14.) Kings are judged good when they fulfill this mandate and evil when they neglect it (Jer. 21:11f., 22:13–17; Mic. 3:9–11).

The distinctive understandings of justice are revealed in the law codes of Israel, especially in their concern for the powerless in the community. Though examining the history and scope of the law codes is beyond the purpose of this essay, I will mention a few things that are important for a biblical foundation of social justice today.

The codes themselves comprise (1) "Covenant Code" (Exod. 20:22–23:33), parts of which date from northern Israel in the ninth century B.C. and reflect premonarchic rural life, though, like the rest of the Pentateuch, it receives its final shape after the exile; (2) the decalogue, found in two versions (Exod. 20:1–17 and Deut. 5:6–21), which represent early covenant law; (3) the Deuteronomic Code (Deut. 12–26), which embodies traditions from the seventh century B.C., and perhaps from Josiah's reform, but which was incorporated into the full-blown "Deuteronomic history" only after the exile; (4) the Holiness Code (Lev. 17–26), put together after the exile and often attributed to priestly circles. This last-mentioned code is also similar to the thought of Ezekiel.

I will confine my comments on the legal texts to those sections that deal with the powerless (often made concrete as the poor, the widow, the orphan, and the stranger in the land).

Norbert Lohfink (whom I follow extensively here) has cautioned against viewing concern for the poor and for others who are powerless as unique to Israel's faith. A survey of a number of Mesopotamian texts (such as the code of Hammurabi) and Egyptian wisdom texts shows a similar concern for *personæ miseræ*, with the exception of care for "the stranger in the land," which is distinctive to Israel. While the content of concern is similar, the foundation and motivation are different. In Israel care for such persons is part of the "contrast society" that is created through the Exodus. Also in Israel this concern functions more as a critical principle against the misuse of power, while in some of the surrounding cultures it is a way in which those in power dampen down revolutionary tendencies of the people and thus maintain a divinely sanctioned hierarchy of power. Also, as Paul Hanson notes, in Israel responsibility for the well-being of such people devolves on the covenant community as a whole and not simply on the king.

Concern for the powerless emerges first as part of the "Covenant Code" (see above). For our purposes, the first important section is Exodus 22:21–27. Here God says, "You shall not wrong or oppress a resident alien, for you were aliens in the land of Egypt" (v. 21; note the motivation of a contrast society). The following verse proscribes abuse of the widow and the orphan, with the promise that God will heed their cry and "kill with the sword" their oppressors; and the section concludes with the prohibition of lending to the poor at interest and the command to restore a neighbor's coat taken in surety for a loan. Here also the motivation is God in his role as the protector of the poor: "And if your neighbor cries out to me, I will listen, for I am compassionate" (Exod. 22:27). The next section contains a series of laws on the proper administration of justice. One of the first states, "You shall not side with the majority so as to pervert justice, nor shall you be partial to the poor in a lawsuit" (Exod. 23:2). The prohibition of "partiality" to the poor in the specific context of a lawsuit does not contradict the concern for the marginal, since v. 6 immediately thereafter commands that "you shall not pervert the justice due to the poor in their lawsuits" (there is no corresponding statement on the rich or powerful), and 23:9 repeats the protection of the alien. In vv. 10f., in a more cultic setting, the code mandates a sabbath year of leaving the land fallow, "so that the poor may eat."

The second major block of legal material dealing with the poor comes from the Deuteronomic legislation of Deut. 12–26. Norbert Lohfink points out that the ideal in the Covenant Code of a contrast society without oppression and poverty was in fact not realized, and locates Deuteronomy in this context. While retaining an ideal that "there will be no one in need among you, because the Lord is sure to bless you" (15:4; see also Acts 4:34), Deuteronomy realistically states, "[T]here will never cease to be some in need on the earth," and commands, "[O]pen your hand to the poor and needy neighbor in the land" (15:11). More strongly than the other codes, Deuteronomy commands justice and compassion for the powerless (Deut. 15:1–18, 24:10–15, 26:11f.). The historical significance of Deuteronomy is that it presents evidence of a continuing concern in Israel's law for the *personæ miseræ*, a concern that attempts to institutionalize the covenant ideal through law and practice. The significance of Deuteronomy in its present canonical location is that it is cast in the form of farewell speeches from Moses to the people on the brink of the promised land. The land is God's gift on condition of fidelity to the covenant ("These are the statutes and ordinances that you must diligently observe in the land the Lord, the God of your ancestors, has given you to occupy" [Deut. 12:1]). When read *after the exile*, it can be seen as a warning against an infidelity that allows the kind of society to develop which is in opposition to the exodus event and the Sinai Covenant.

The Holiness Code (Lev. 17–26) contains provisions similar to Deuteronomy. In 19:9f. and 23:22 gleanings from the harvest are to be left for "the poor and the alien," though, as Lohfink points out, specific mention is not made of "the widow and the orphan," who now seem to be subsumed under "the poor." The Holiness Code has spelled out in detail other provisions for the poor, very often for those who have come suddenly upon hard times (Lev. 25:35–42, 47–52). Leviticus is also more concerned with the details of repayment of debts and cultic offerings made by the poor (Lev. 12:8=Luke 2:24). The significance of Leviticus is twofold. First, though it is primarily a cultic code concerned with the holiness of the people and the means to assure that holiness, it manifests a practical concern for the poor of the land. As John Gammie has shown in his excellent study, there is no tension between Israel's concern to be a holy people, consecrated to God, and a people concerned about justice. Secondly, and perhaps less positively, Leviticus seems to represent a relaxation of some of the earlier provisions for the poor. Lohfink argues that the stipulations of the Jubilee (Lev. 25:8–17, 23–25; 27:16–25), where debts are canceled every fiftieth year, would hardly benefit the majority of people who lived in poverty, and that they represent a step back from the sabbath-year legislation of Deuteronomy. The Holiness Code may also reflect the radically changed postexilic political situation, when the monarchy was extinct and people had a limited ability to enshrine the ideals of the covenant in law. This period also represents the beginning of apocalyptic thought, when many groups took their hope of God's justice and a society free of oppression and poverty and projected it toward a new heaven and a new earth that would be ushered in by cosmic cataclysm.

The events of salvation history, especially the Exodus from Egypt and the covenant at Sinai, are thus the foundations in Israel of a society that seeks justice and manifests concern for the marginal. This concern is incorporated in law and custom, which take different shapes in different historical circumstances, stretching over five centuries. As founding documents not only of the historical people of Israel but of the Christian Church, they offer a vision of life in society before God that is to inform religious belief and social practice. The laws of Israel have two great values. First, they show that religious belief must be translated into law and custom which guide life in community and protect the vulnerable. Paul Hanson states this well in describing *Torah* as "faith coming to expression in communal forms and structures" (*The People Called*, 47). Second, although these traditions do not offer concrete directives for our complex socioeconomic world, they offer a vision of a "contrast society" not ruled by power and greed, where the treatment of the marginal becomes the touchstone of "right relationship" to God. Christians and Jesuits today must ask soberly how our lives provide a contrast society and whether, when we think of our "right relation" to God, the concerns of the marginal in our own time have been really made concrete in our attitudes and style of life.

In working with the project of "Preaching the Just Word," over the last decade participants frequently ask about the difference between "biblical justice" and other forms of justice rooted in the philosophical tradition (commutative justice, distributive justice, social justice). A few comments may be helpful.

1. I have already indicated that biblical justice does not admit of strict philosophical definition, but in the texts themselves is often linked with qualities such as "mercy," "steadfast love," and "fidelity." The traditional contrast between obligations in charity and obligations in justice is foreign to the Bible. Jesus expresses this in Matthew by criticizing the Pharisees for neglecting the weightier things of the law—"justice and mercy and faith" (Matt 23:23 [NRSV]).

2. Biblical justice is fundamentally "making things right," not simply recognizing or defining *individual rights*. It is concerned with the "right relation" of human beings to God and to each other. There is no conflict between the "vertical dimension," that is, the proper relationship to God and God's commands and the "horizontal dimension," the need to structure social life in a way that respects human dignity and is concerned for the vulnerable in the community. Jesus expresses this through the dual command of love of God and neighbor (Mark 12:28–34, Matt. 22:15–22, Luke 20:20–26).

3. Biblical justice is not "blind," nor totally impartial. It is partial to those most affected by evil and oppression—symbolized in the Old Testament by the four groups of widows, orphans, the poor, and strangers in the land, and embodied in the NT by Jesus' mission to those on the social and religious margin of society. There are "two women of justice," one with a scale and her eyes blinded, and the other, who proclaims: "[H]e has shown might with his arm, dispersed the arrogant of mind and heart. He has thrown down rulers from their thrones, but lifted up the lowly. The hungry he has filled with good things, the rich he has sent away empty" (Luke 1:51–53).

Bibliography on Covenant, Law, and the Meaning of Justice

See also Ogletree, *Use of the Bible,* 47–86, for an excellent discussion of covenant and moral life.

Ahern, Barnabas M. "Biblical Doctrine on the Rights and Duties of Man." *Gregorianum* 65 (1984): 301–17.

*Berkovits, Eliezer. "The Biblical Meaning of Justice." *Judaism* 18 (1969): 188–209. A good survey by a Jewish scholar very sensitive to the nuances of meaning in the different Hebrew terms.

+Bovati, Pietro. *Re-establishing Justice: Legal Terms, Concepts and Procedures in the Hebrew Bible.* Translated by Michael J. Smith. In *Journal for the Study of the Old Testament.* Supplement series no. 105. Sheffield: JSOT Press, 1994. Comprehensive and foundational study.

Donahue, John R. "Biblical Perspectives on Justice." In *The Faith That Does Justice.* New York/Ramsey: Paulist Press, 1977.

Biale, David. "Jewish Statements on Social Justice." In *A Cry for Justice,* ed. R. M. Brown and S. Thompson, 64–77. New York: Paulist Press, 1989. It covers biblical and contemporary statements. See also these essays: J. Coleman, "A New Catholic Vision of Social Justice," and Karen Lebacqz, "Protestant Statements on Economic Justice."

Epsztein, Léon. *Social Justice in the Ancient Near East and the People of the Bible.* London: SCM Press, 1986. Good on background of Israel's social legislation.

+Fitzmyer, J. A. "What Do the Scriptures Say about Justice?" Lecture at the Conference "Jesuit Education 21" at St. Joseph's University, June 26, 1999. Fitzmyer presents a careful philological discussion of the Hebrew and Greek terms for justice, then concentrates on the Pauline use of justice/justification, and offers brief comments on the application of biblical understandings of justice to Church life today. This paper with responses by biblical scholars Richard Clifford, Stanley Marrow, and Mark Smith will be published by St. Joseph's University Press as "Proceedings of the Jesuit Education 21 Conference," ed. Martin Tripole. It is expected to appear in April 2000.

*Gammie, John G. *Holiness in Israel.* Minneapolis: Fortress Press, 1989. This is the best study in English on holiness. Gammie surveys holiness in the priestly, prophetic, wisdom, and apocalyptic traditions and writes with great sensitivity to contemporary religious and social concerns.

*Gnuse, Robert. *You Shall Not Steal: Community and Property in the Biblical Tradition.* Maryknoll, N.Y.: Orbis, 1985. Gnuse is primarily an OT scholar. This well-researched and well-written work traces the biblical attitude toward possessions from the earliest law codes down through the NT.

*Hanson, Paul D. *The People Called: The Growth of Community in the Bible.* San Francisco: Harper and Row, 1986. This is really a complete biblical theology seen through the lens of different understandings of community in the historical evolution of Israel (through the NT). "Community" for

Hanson always involves a triad of worship, compassion, and righteous-ness. Hanson is very sensitive to issues of social justice.

+ ———. "The Ancient Jewish Near Eastern Roots of Social Welfare." In *Through the Eye of a Needle: Judeo-Christian Roots of Social Welfare,* ed. Emily Alb Hanawalt and Carter Lindberg, 7–28. Kirksville, Mo.: Thomas Jefferson University Press, 1997. A good concise overview of important texts.

Harrelson, Walter. *The Ten Commandments and Human Rights.* Philadelphia: Fortress Press, 1980; *[Addition]* repr. Macon, Ga.: Mercer University Press, 1997. One of the most helpful writings on the relation of the decalogue to all aspects of Israel's life, with strong sensitivity to ques-tions of social justice today.

Hillers, Delbert R. *Covenant: The History of a Biblical Idea.* Baltimore: Johns Hopkins University Press, 1969.

+ Johnson, Barbara. *"Mišpāt."* In *Theological Dictionary of the Old Testament,* 9 (1998): 86–98; *"Saedeq, Sedaqah, Saddiq."* In *Theologisches Wörter-buch zum Alten Testament,* svv; an English translation of this, entitled *Theological Dictionary,* is soon to appear. Excellent articles which should be foundation of future reflection.

+ Knierem, Rolf P. "Justice in Old Testament Theology." In *The Task of Old Testament Theology: Substance Method and Cases,* 86–122. Grand Rapids: Eerdmans, 1992.

*Lohfink, Norbert. *Option for the Poor: The Basic Principle of Liberation Theol-ogy in Light of the Bible.* The Bailey Lectures. Edited by D. Christiansen. Berkeley: Bibal Press, 1986. Order from American Baptist Seminary of the West, 2515 Hillengass Ave., Berkeley, Cal. 94704. The book treats both legal and prophetic texts, but is listed here because it offers fundamental perspectives on issues of justice for the poor; it is short and written in a lively style.

———. "Poverty in the Laws of the Ancient Near East and the Bible." *Theo-logical Studies* 52 (1991): 34–50. The best single thing on the poor in Israel's evolving legal traditions.

McCarthy, Dennis J. *Old Testament Covenant: A Survey of Current Opinions.* Atlanta: John Knox Press, 1972. The best survey of current opinions on covenant.

Malchow, Bruce V. "Social Justice in the Israelite Law Codes." In *Word and World* 4, no. 3 (1984): 293–306. Clear and readable overview.

+ ———. *Social Justice in the Hebrew Bible.* Collegeville, Minn.: Liturgical Press, 1996. Good short overview; good for class use or with parish discussion group.

Menzes, Ruiz de, "Social Justice in Israel's Law." In *Bible Bhashyam* 11, nos. 1 and 2 (March–June 1985): 10–46. The best comprehensive and short survey of social concerns in the legal traditions. (Note: Many interesting and important articles that relate the Bible and social justice are being published in the two Indian journals *Bible Bhashyam* and *Vidyajoti.* Librari-ans take note!)

Miranda, José. *Marx and the Bible.* Maryknoll, N.Y.: Orbis, 1974). Despite the title, which may seem both naive and dated, Miranda provides evocative and challenging perspectives on many important texts.

+ Nardoni, E. *Los que buscan la justicia: Un estudio de las justicia en el mundo biblico.* Estella, Navarra: Editorial Verbo Divino, 1997.

+ Murray, Robert. *The Cosmic Covenant: Biblical Themes of Justice, Peace and the Integrity of Creation.* Heythrop Monographs, no. 7. London: Sheed & Ward, 1992. Important study by a British Jesuit on the relation of justice to themes of creation with implications for ecology.

+ *Reventlow, H. G., and Y. Hoffman, eds. *Justice and Righteousness: Biblical Themes and Their Influence.* In *Journal for the Study of the Old Testament,* Supplementary Series, no. 137. Sheffield, Eng: JSOT Press, 1992. A very fine collection of essays including, C. Frey, *"The Impact of the Biblical Idea of Justice on Present Discussions of Social Justice"; Moshe Weinfeld, *'Justice and Righteousness'—*mishpatim wetseadakah:* The Expression and Its Meaning."

+ Scaria, K. J. "Social Justice in the Old Testament." In *Bible Bhashyam* 4 (1978): 163–92. An excellent overview by a seminary professor in Kerala.

+ Stuhlmueller, Carroll. "Prophet-Mystic and Social Justice: An Exploration." In *Biblical Research* 36 (1991): 35–60, with replies by Pauline Viviano and R. W. Klein. An important article addressing the neglect of the relation between prophets' religious experience and social commitment.

* Walsh, J. P. M. *The Mighty from Their Thrones.* Philadelphia: Fortress Press, 1987. This could be listed under different headings. It is a theology of Israel's history and traditions, with stress on the marginal as the bearers of God's promises.

+ Weinfeld, Moshe. *Social Justice in Ancient Israel and in the Ancient Near East.* Minneapolis, Minn.: Fortress Press; Jerusalem: Magnes, 1995.

The Prophetic Concern for the Poor and Powerless

Let me precede this section with a word about *terminology.* The focus of this survey is on those writings that speak of concern for the marginal or powerless, often described globally as "the poor." The biblical tradition has a number of words for the poor. At the risk of seeming overly technical, I will indicate five of these.

1. *'ānî* (plural, *'ăniyyîm*) probably derives from a root *'nh,* meaning "bent down" or "afflicted"; it occurs eighty times in the OT; in the Greek translation of the OT (=LXX), it is translated by *ptōchos* (beggar or destitute person) thirty-eight times, by *penēs* or *penichros* (needy person) thirteen times, by *tapeinos* (lowly; see also Luke 1:52) nine times, or by *praüs* (gentle) four times.

2. *'ānāw* (plural *'ănāwîm*), derived from the same root as *'ānî* and often confused by copyists (for example, at Qumran), is used twenty-five times; it is most often translated by *tapeinos* and *praüs* (humble and lowly), but also by *ptōchos* and *penēs*.

3. *'ebyôn* (the term "Ebionites" derives from this), whose root is a very debated question, comes from a word meaning "lack" or "need" or "wretched," miserable"; it is used sixty-one times in the OT (especially twenty-three times in Psalms) and appears often in a stereotyped formula with *'ānî;* for example, in Deut. 24:14; Jer. 22:16; Eze. 16:49, 18:12, 22:29; it is translated by the LXX as *penēs* twenty-nine times, as *ptōchos* ten times, and as *adynatos* (powerless) four times.

4. *dal,* coming from a term meaning "be bent over," "bent down," or "miserable," is used forty-eight times; and the LXX translates it as *ptōchos* twenty-three times, as *penēs/penichros* ten times, as *asthenēs* (weak or sick) five times. It is also used in synonymous parallelism with *'ānî* (Isa. 10:2, 26:6; Zeph. 3:12; Pss. 72:13, 82:3; Job 34:28; Prov. 22:22) and *'ebyôn* (1 Sam. 2:8; Isa. 14:30; Amos 2:7, 4:1, 5:11; Pss. 72:13, 82:4, 113:7).

5. *rāš* means "poor" in a derogatory sense, with overtones of a lazy person responsible for his or her own poverty. It is not found in the Pentateuch or Prophets, but in the Wisdom literature (for example, Prov. 10:4, 13:23, 14:20, 19:7, 28:3).

The New Testament vocabulary is not as rich, using almost exclusively *ptōchos* about thirty-five times; for *penēs,* see 1 Cor. 9:9; for *penichros,* Luke 21:2; for *tapeinos,* Luke 1:52; Matt. 11:29; Rom. 12:16; James 1:9, 4:6.

The importance of the terminology is twofold. First, it shows that "poverty" was not itself a value. Even etymologically the poor are bent down, wretched, and beggars. While the Bible has great concern for "the poor," poverty itself is an evil. Second, the terminology (as well as the actual use) is a caution against misuse of the phrase "spiritually poor." Though later literature (the Psalms and Qumran) often equate the poor with the humble or meek and though the poor are those people open to God, in contrast to idolatrous or blind rich people, the "prime analogue" of the term is an economic condition. When the "poor in spirit" are praised, as in Matt. 5:3, it is because, in addition to their material poverty, they are open to God's presence and love. Certain contemporary usages of "spiritual poverty," which allow it to be used of extremely wealthy people who are unhappy even amid prosperity, are not faithful to the biblical tradition. Nor is an idea of "spiritual poverty" as indifference to riches amid wealth faithful to the Bible. The "poor" in the Bible are almost without exception powerless people who experience economic and social deprivation (see especially the article by Soares Prabhu).

The Prophets and the Call for Justice

When a people forget their origins or lose sight of the ideals, figures arise who often speak a strident message to summon them to return to God. In Israel's history the prophetic movement represents such a phenomenon. The prophet, as the Greek etymology of the name suggests (*pro-phēmi*), speaks on behalf of another. This has a dual sense. The prophet speaks on behalf of God; he or she is a "forth teller," one who also speaks on behalf of those who have no one to speak for them, specifically, the powerless and poor in the land.

Like all topics treated in this essay, prophecy is a minefield of historical and literary problems, so I will limit my reflections to a few introductory comments and then highlight some prophetic texts (now quite familiar to most Jesuits) that bear on the faith that does justice.

For many decades the social teaching of Israel was virtually identified with the prophetic message. There is a danger in this when prophetic religion was often contrasted to a religion of law or was seen as a criticism of all cultic activity. The reduction of the religion of Israel to prophetic ethics often fostered an undercurrent of anti-Semitism, since postbiblical Judaism was and remains heavily centered on *Torah*. The attitude developed among some Christian scholars that the Judaism after the prophets was a decline into legalism. Also the somewhat naive interpretation of the prophets as anticultic was often seen as justification for the reduction of religious life to social activism or a neglect of communal liturgical life.

Recent research on the prophets has underscored a number of considerations of importance in assessing the prophetic texts that I will list below.

1. The prophets are generally "conservative" in the best sense of the word. They hark back to the originating experiences of Israel to counter the corrupting influences of urbanization and centralized power that developed under the monarchy, especially after the split between the northern kingdom (Israel) and the southern kingdom (Judea) following the death of Solomon (922 B.C.). Their works are also a collection of traditions, some going back to the originally named prophets, others additions by disciples and later editors. Much recent research has attempted to describe these levels of tradition.

2. The prophets are not opposed to cultic worship, but to its corruption. Jeremiah was the son of a priest, Isaiah used cultic imagery associ-

ated with the Jerusalem temple, and Ezekiel was steeped in the cult. Recent research on Amos, often popularly portrayed as a "righteous peasant," has suggested some contact with the Jerusalem temple.

3. In assessing the prophetic texts on justice and concern for the marginal, we must give careful attention to the literary context of a given text, but—what is even more important—to its historical context as well. Amos, for example, prophesied at the northern court shortly before the fall of Samaria to the Assyrians (721 B.C.). During this time, however, the northern kingdom experienced material prosperity. Under Solomon's rule a more prosperous upper class had emerged. This created a class with a vested interest in the accumulation of land and goods as capital. The old emphasis disappeared that regarded the land as the inheritance of every Israelite (see 1 Kings 21, the story of Naboth's vineyard). James L. Mays describes this as "the shift of the primary social good, land, from the function of support to that of capital; the reorientation of social goals from personal values to personal profit; to subordination of judicial process to the interests of the entrepreneur" ("Justice," 9). Amos's harsh words against the prosperous must be set in this context.

Isaiah of Jerusalem (Isa. 1–39) flourishes roughly during the same period. His political message to the southern kings is to avoid the kinds of political entanglement that would ultimately spell the downfall of the northern kingdom. Though Isaiah is eloquent on the demand for justice, his motivation is different from those of Amos or Hosea. The controlling principle of much of Isaiah's teaching was his conviction of the holiness and kingly power of God. Oppression of the weaker members of the community offended Yahweh's holiness, so Isaiah vehemently criticizes injustice (see below).

4. Though the prophets criticize the misuse of power by those in authority, their message is reformist rather than revolutionary. They do not envision a community without a king or without laws and statutes. During the greatest part bulk of the postexilic period—especially after the codification of the law under Ezra and Nehemiah, when the people lack their own kings and live under the successive rule of the Persians, under the successors of Alexander, and finally under the Romans— prophecy as a movement within Judaism virtually ceases. Biblical prophecy required a heritage of values shared by the rulers and the ruled, even when those in power did not live up to these values. When a people have no control over their destiny and are subject to brutal power, prophecy can take the form only of protest, not of a call to reform.

Principal Prophetic Texts That Deal with Justice and Concern for the Marginal

Pre-exilic Prophetic Texts

Amos (c. 750 B.C.: from the south [Tekoa], he prophesied in the north against Israel). *Texts:* Amos 2:6–4:13 (strong criticisms of the lifestyle and exploitative practices of the upper classes); 5:10–6:14 (summons to justice and conversion).

Isaiah (between 740–701 B.C. in Jerusalem, during the reigns of Uzziah, Jotham, Ahaz, and Hezekiah; see 2 Kings 14:23–20:20). *Texts:* Criticism of injustice: 1:10–17, 21–26; 3:13–15; 5:1–10, 20–23; 10:1–4; 32:6f. Isaiah also criticizes false religion (1:12–17; see Isa. 58) and calls God the "stronghold of the poor" (25:5). In his eschatological section he looks to a time when the meek will obtain fresh joy in the Lord and the poor will exult in the holy one of Israel (29:19f.; see Matt. 5:3f.). Yet Isaiah speaks of the power of conversion (1:18f., 26f.) and of hope in an ideal king (2:2–4, 9:1–7, 11:1–9).

Micah (c. 725–701 B.C. from Moresheth in Judah; he attacked the Jerusalem leaders). *Texts:* 2:1–11, 3:9–12, 5:3–8 (note especially the recollection of Exod. 7:1–3). "The prophet knows at firsthand about the expulsion of small landholders from their traditional means of livelihood, dishonest business practices, venal priests and prophets, and a royal regime that connives in the oppression of the poor."[4]

Hosea (fl. c. 745–721), the sole "writing prophet" from the north. More than the "southern" prophets, he draws on the early traditions of Israel, but contains few sayings dealing with social ills. Hosea speaks against idolatry and syncretism and summons the people to return to the first love they experienced from God in the wilderness. Apart from the covenant formulation mentioned above (Hos. 2:19–21), only his summons to Ephraim in 10:12–14, to "sow for yourselves righteousness," and his criticism of their trust in "your power and in the multitude of your warriors" (10:13) reflect social concerns found in the other prophets.

Jeremiah (c. 626–586 B.C.), prophet of Josiah's (639–609) Deuteronomistic reform (2 Kings 23); his historical context was one of turmoil. *Texts:* Jer. 5:20–31, especially v. 28; 22:13–17.

---

[4] N. Gottwald, *The Hebrew Bible: A Socio-Literary Introduction* (Philadelphia: Fortress Press, 1985), 375.

Zephaniah (from reign of Josiah, 640–609). *Text:* Zeph. 3:11–13; the importance of this text is that it pronounces the whole people as the "poor and lowly."

Exilic and Postexilic Prophetic Texts

Ezekiel (593–571 B.C.). *Texts:* 16:49, 18:5–18, 22:28–31, 34:1–31.

Deutero-Isaiah (Isa. 40–55) and Trito-Isaiah (Isa. 56–66). The oracles of Deutero-Isaiah seem to date from the period just before 539 B.C., that is, the restoration under Cyrus, while Trito-Isaiah reflects the postexilic period. *Texts:* Isa. 41:17, 51:21–23, 58:1–9 (the true fast), 61:1–7 (see Luke 4:16–19), 66:2.

Zechariah (c. 520–18 B.C.). *Text:* 7:8–14.

▶ ◀

Bibliographies on the Poor and the Prophets

The Poor

See also the works of Lohfink, p. 44 below.

Articles in the *Theological Dictionary of the Old Testament.* Edited by G. J. Botterwick and H. Ringgren. Grand Rapids: Eerdmans, 1977–.: *>ebyôn* 1:27–41; *dal* 3:208–30; and, in the *Theological Dictionary of the New Testament, ptōchos* 6:885–915. See also "The Poor," in *Harpers Bible Dictionary,* 807f.

Fensham, F. C. "Widow, Orphan and the Poor in Ancient Near Eastern Legal and Wisdom Literature." *Journal of Near Eastern Studies* 21 (1962): 129–39.

Furman, Frida K. "The Prophetic Tradition and Social Transformation." In *Prophetic Visions and Economic Realities: Protestants, Jews and Catholics Confront the Bishops' Letter on the Economy,* ed. C. Strain, 103–14. Grand Rapids: Eerdmans, 1989. A good survey of ways the prophetic tradition has been used.

Gelin, Albert. *The Poor of Yahweh.* Collegeville: Liturgical Press, 1964. A "classic" on the poor in the Bible, with coverage of major texts, but with a tendency toward "spiritualization" of poverty.

*George, A., ed. *Gospel Poverty: Essays in Biblical Theology.* Chicago: Franciscan Herald Press, 1977. A very important collection of essays by leading French biblical scholars. The essays by George on the OT and Dupont on the NT are especially good.

Gowan, D. "Wealth and Poverty in the Old Testament: The Case of the Widow, the Orphan and the Sojourner." *Interpretation* 41 (1987): 341–53.

Guinan, M. D. *Gospel Poverty: Witness to the Risen Christ.* New York/Ramsey: Paulist Press, 1981. Survey of the theme of poverty in OT, Qumran, and NT, with stress on how poverty becomes a witness to the risen Christ. Good for pastoral use.

Hoppe, Leslie J. *Being Poor: A Biblical Study.* Wilmington, Del.: Michael Glazier, 1987. A fine study of important texts.

Johnson, Luke T. *Sharing Possessions: Mandate and Symbol of Faith.* Philadelphia: Fortress Press, 1981. An excellent study of a wide range of biblical texts. Very good on symbolic meaning of possessions in the Bible.

Patterson, R. "The Widow, the Orphan and the Poor in the Old Testament and Extra-biblical Literature." *Bibliotheca Sacra* 130 (1973): 223–35.

Soares-Prabhu, G. "Class in the Bible: The Biblical Poor a Social Class?" *Vidyajoti* 49 (1985): 322–46. He rejects interpretation of poor in religious terms alone.

The Prophets

Achtemeier, Paul J., and James L. Mays, eds. *Interpreting the Prophets.* Philadelphia: Fortress Press, 1987. A series of articles originally published in *Interpretation.* They treat mainly literary and historical problems, with the essays on Jeremiah by Brueggemann and Holladay particularly helpful, as is the "Resources for Studying the Prophets" by J. Limburg.

+Berquist, Jon L. "Dangerous Waters of Justice and Righteousness: Amos 5:18–27." *Biblical Theology Bulletin* 23 (1993) 54–63.

*Brueggemann, Walter. *The Prophetic Imagination.* Philadelphia: Fortress Press, 1978. A very influential and readable interpretation of the prophets.

Blenkinsopp, Joseph. *A History of Prophecy in Israel.* Philadelphia: Westminster Press, 1983. One of the best standard introductions to all aspects of the prophets.

Coote, Robert. *Amos among the Prophets: Composition and Theology.* Philadelphia: Fortress Press, 1981. A very interesting and challenging view of Amos, with strong emphasis on his social teaching.

+Dempsey, Carol. J. *The Prophets: A Liberation-Critical Reading.* Minneapolis, Minn.: Fortress, 2000.

+Doorly, William J. *Prophet of Justice*: *Understanding the Book of Amos.* New York/Mahwah, N.J.: Paulist, 1989.

+Gossai, Hemchand. *Justice, Righteousness, and the Social Critique of the Eighth-century Prophets.* American University Studies. Series VII, Theology and Religion. New York: P. Lang, 1993.

Heschel, Abraham. *The Prophets.* 2 vols. Harper Torchbooks. New York: Harper and Row, 1962. A very original and interesting reading of the prophets, with strong emphasis on their religious experience.

+Leclerc, Thomas. "*Mišpāt* Justice) in the Book of Isaiah." Ph.D. dissertation. Harvard University, 1998 (under Paul Hanson). Excellent study of Isaiah arguing for strong social justice bent of First Isaiah.

Limburg, James. *The Prophets and the Powerless.* Atlanta: John Knox Press, 1977. A helpful and readable study.

*Mays, James L. "Justice: Perspectives from the Prophetic Tradition." In *Prophecy in Israel,* ed. D. Petersen, 144–58 (see next entry). A concise and well-written summary of prophetic concern for justice; also in *Interpretation* 37 (1983): 5–17.

Petersen, David L., ed. *Prophecy in Israel: Search for an Identity.* Philadelphia: Fortress Press, 1987. A collection of classic (by Gunkel, Mowinckel, and Weber) and recent articles on the prophets. The introduction by Petersen is a good statement of contemporary research on the prophets.

Reid, David P. *What Are They Saying about the Prophets?* New York/Mahwah: Paulist Press, 1980. A good survey of research, but not a great deal on justice and the prophets. Good bibliography.

*Sklba, Richard J. *Pre-exilic Prophecy: Message of Biblical Spirituality.* A Michael Glazier Book. Collegeville: Liturgical Press, 1990. A very fine study of the prophets, organized thematically. The section "Voices for the Poor" is very helpful.

Wilson, Robert. *Prophecy and Society in Ancient Israel.* Philadelphia: Fortress Press, 1980. A scholarly and important study on the social setting of the prophets.

Israel after the Exile: A New Situation

Above I alluded to significant changes in Israelite life after the Babylonian exile: deportation of upper classes to Babylon (597 B.C.,); other deportations (587 and 582 B.C.); return under Cyrus (539 B.C.). The subsequent period is generally divided into the Persian period (539–332) and the Hellenistic Period (332–175), followed by a brief period of independence under the Hasmonean kings (175–163), which yielded to Roman rule either under client kings (Herod and his sons) or Roman prefects (in Judea). This period also witnessed the rise of a large corpus of "intertestamental writings" (Apocrypha and Pseudepigrapha) which are important for the history of ideas and as a background to the NT, even though most are not part of the Jewish and Christian canon.

With conscious oversimplification, I would like to highlight three considerations in regard to concern for the poor. First, during this period the sense of individual responsibility develops (Ezek. 18:1–32, 33:1–20), with the consequent focus on the justice or right relation of the individual to God. Second, there is the expansion of "apocalyptic" literature. Here the hope for God's saving justice is removed from history and reserved for the end of history, when the wicked will be punished and the just rewarded. Allied to this are attacks with increasing invective and vehemence against the wealthy (for example, 1 Enoch 92–105). The third consideration is the expansion of "wisdom literature";

for example, the Wisdom of Solomon and Ben Sirach (Ecclesiasticus), couched in the form of maxims or sayings, many of which describe how to survive and succeed in everyday life. This literature shows a much stronger influence of Hellenism than the apocalyptic literature and may originate among the growing number of city dwellers engaged in commerce and in the governmental bureaucracy. Alexander DiLella, for example, suggests that, were he living today, Ben Sirach might have an appointment in a business school. Such complex social developments in postexilic Israel would explain the seemingly contradictory attitudes toward wealth and poverty characterizing this period.

Again, riding the tide of oversimplification, I would like to propose a few summary statements on rich and poor in the Bible.

1. The "poor" are primarily the sociologically poor. They are the economically destitute and the socially outcast, typified by the characteristic biblical figures of exploited powerlessness—the widow, the orphan, and the refugee (Soares-Prabhu, "Class in the Bible," 326). In contemporary parlance the poor would better be described as "the powerless."

2. The poor have a special claim on the community and its leaders; they are "just" because they do not follow the evil ways of the rich and powerful. Both the king and the whole people are obliged to seek justice, which involves being on the side of the poor and the powerless. This perspective informs all of Israel's traditions in all stages of its history.

3. Riches are both a danger and an evil. Often they are associated with idolatry and oppressions (see especially Ps. 10). They present a temptation to secure one's life apart from God (see Luke 12:13–21) or cause blindness in the face of the needy neighbor (Luke 16:19–31). Compare the standard of Satan in the *Spiritual Exercises:* "the lust of riches," "the empty honor of the world," and "unbounded pride."

Selection of Texts Showing the Status of the Poor in the Postexilic Period

Psalms 10; 34:6; 37:14; 41:1; 69:33; **72:1, 4, 12–14;** 82:1–4; 109:16–22; 112:9; 113:7; 132:14. At times in the psalms the poor are identified with the humble or those open to God. They are, however, subject to oppression and persecution by the wicked and the greedy (see especially Ps. 10). They are examples of the economically poor who are also spiritually poor, in the sense of placing their hope in God.

Proverbs. Different strains are present:

1. Poverty is an evil brought about by humans (usually by sloth): Prov. 6:9–11 (=24:33f.); 10:4, 15; 20:13; 21:17; 23:21.

2. It is a misfortune to be poor: 10:15, 13:8, 14:20, 19:4, 19:7, 19:22, 22:7, 28:3, 30:8f.

3. The poor are victimized by the powerful: 10:15, 13:23, 18:23, 22:7, 28:15, 30:13f.

4. God is "on the side of" the poor and wants justice for them: 14:31, 17:5, 19:17, 21:13, 22:2, 22:9, 22:22f., 28:27, 29:14, 31:9.

5. Riches can be evil and poverty can foster righteousness: 16:19; 19:1; 19:22; 22:16; 28:6; 28:11; 29:7; 31:9, 20.

Ben Sirach (also called *Ecclesiasticus*) was written about 180 B.C. in Jerusalem by an instructor of wealthy youths; it was translated into Greek about 132 B.C. by the author's grandson. *Texts* which continue concern for the poor: 4:1–10; 7:32; 10:19–11:1; 21:5; 29:9, 22; 30:14; 31:1–11; 34:20–22; 35:13–20; 38:19; *Texts* that have a negative view of the poor: 13:3f., 19–23; 18:32f.; 25:2.

▶ ◀

Bibliography on the Poor in Psalms, Wisdom Literature, and Other Postexilic Literature

See also the general studies above, many of which cover this literature.

+ Bergant, Dianne. *Israel's Wisdom Literature: A Liberation-Critical Reading.* Minneapolis, Minn.: Fortress, 1997.

+ Ceresko, Anthony. *Introduction to Old Testament Wisdom: A Spirituality for Liberation.* Maryknoll, N.Y.: Orbis, 1999.

Gillingham, Sue. "The Poor in the Psalms." *Expository Times* 100 (1989): 15–19.

Klein, Ralph W. *Israel in Exile.* Philadelphia: Fortress Press, 1979. A fine study of theological responses to the experience of exile. "Exile" is an experience and theological category that merits more study on issues of faith and justice.

Malchow, Bruce. "Social Justice in the Wisdom Literature." *Biblical Theological Bulletin* 12 (1982): 120–24.

Nickelsburg, George W. "Riches, the Rich, and God's Judgment in 1 Enoch 92–105 and the Gospel According to Luke." *New Testament Studies* 25 (1978–79): 324–44. 1 Enoch is really an apocalypse, but I have listed this study here as indicative of a postexilic perspective.

Pleins, J. D. "Poverty in the Social World of the Wise." *Journal for the Study of the Old Testament* 37 (1987): 61–78.

Schmidt, T. Ewald. "Hostility to Wealth in Philo of Alexandria." *Journal for the Study of the New Testament* 19 (1983): 85–97. I have added this for the sake of historical completeness, since Philo represents an important voice in diaspora Judaism of the first century A.D.

Schuller, Eileen. *Post-exilic Prophets.* A Michael Glazier Book. Collegeville: Liturgical Press, 1988. Good on historical setting and theology of the postexilic prophets.

Whybray, R. N. *Wealth and Poverty in the Book of Proverbs.* Sheffield: JSPT, 1990.

———. "Poverty, Wealth, and Point of View in Proverbs." *Expository Times* 100 (1988–89): 332–36.

THE NEW TESTAMENT

Introduction

The canonical NT books emerged in less than a century; and their social, political, and cultural contexts were far less diverse than those of the OT and intertestamental literature. Yet many Christians today are somewhat like the second-century heretic Marcion, who rejected the OT; they often want to ground their ethics in the NT, to the neglect of the Hebrew Scriptures. I will select five areas of consideration where there have been significant discussions of issues lending themselves to questions of social justice. This means that the Gospel and letters of John are overlooked. Though there are significant sections, especially 1 John 3:11–18, that bear directly on issues of social justice, the Johannine writings thus far have not been the subject of intense discussion by those interested in NT social ethics. The areas I will deal with are (1) the teaching and ministry of Jesus, (2) Jewish Christianity as manifest in the Gospel of Matthew and in the Letter of James, (3) the Gospel of Luke and the Acts of the Apostles, (4) the letters of Paul, and (5) the Book of Revelation.

The Teaching and Ministry of Jesus

While it is axiomatic to say that Jesus was not a social reformer, his teachings and actions had strong social implications during his lifetime and continue to shape the consciences of his followers today. A key to his life is his use of either explicit terms or parables to proclaim the imminence of God's reign or kingdom. He also brings about the kingdom by performing acts of power (healings and exorcisms) and by associating with and offering God's love to "the marginal" of his day, especially tax collectors and sinners.

Many scholars today locate Jesus' teaching in the wider context of different "restorationist" movements alive in Palestine. Jesus is seen as summoning people to a renewed dedication to the primacy of God in their lives and to a deepened concern for their neighbor (the dual command of love). This command of love is made perfect in love and forgiveness of one's enemies. The God disclosed by Jesus makes his sun shine on the good and the bad. Jesus' teaching breaks down the penchant people have for dividing the world into clearly identifiable friends and enemies, outsiders and insiders.

Like many of his contemporaries, Jesus hoped for the intervention of God in history in the near future (imminent eschatology), yet he proclaimed that the reign of God had already begun in his teaching and action and that people were to live in response to it (eschatology in the process of realization). The eschatological thrust of Jesus' teaching (and later of Paul's) should not be invoked to undermine its effective impact (as if the nearness of the end made ethical behavior superfluous); rather it is "a view from the future" of what life should be in the present. That God's definitive reign is still in the future does not dispense us from living according to its norms and values in our everyday lives.

Jesus' teaching is a summons to a conversion that is to affect the way people live in the world. In Matthew's version of the Lord's Prayer (6:9f.), Jesus prays that God's will be done and God's kingdom come *on earth*. In the beatitudes, which are also in the Q source, with high claims of authenticity, Jesus calls the poor and the oppressed "blessed," not because their actual condition is such, but because the kingdom that he proclaims and enacts will confront those values and conditions that have made them marginal. This was the great value of the massive studies of Jacques Dupont on the beatitudes that are summarized in the essay mentioned above (in George, *Gospel Poverty*). In all levels of this teaching, from the early Q source through the Lucan writings, response to the kingdom demands complete reliance on God rather than on power or wealth.

The kingdom as proclaimed by Jesus challenged the deep-seated expectations of his hearers. This is especially true in his parables, which contain frequent reversals; for example, those who worked only one hour received the same wage as those who had worked all day; Jesus says that one should invite not friends but unknown strangers gathered from the highways to a banquet; the hated outsider, a Samaritan, teaches the true meaning of love of neighbor; the prodigal is accepted as readily as the dutiful. These reversals challenge deeply held values and invite people to enter imaginatively into a different world, providing a paradigm for the manner in which a new vision of social justice can be presented to people today. (See especially Michael Cook, *Jesus' Parables.*)

Jesus' acceptance of marginal groups counters the evaluation of people by class and social status that was characteristic of first-century society. Also, by associating with those seen as ritually unclean and by being willing to break the law on their behalf, Jesus alienates the religious establishment of his day in such a way that he is both a political and a religious threat. By taking the side of these people, Jesus, like the OT prophets, gives a voice to the voiceless. Ultimately, Jesus dies a victim of a form of execution reserved for those who were threats to the "public order," owing to collusion between the Jerusalem temple authorities (whose power rested on proper subservience to Rome) and the Roman prefect, Pontius Pilate. Jesus' life is a paradigm of the cost of discipleship for those who take the side of the poor and the marginal. On Nov. 16, 1989, our Jesuit brothers and their co-workers in San Salvador again proclaimed this cost to the world.

Bibliography on the Life and Teaching of Jesus

Before beginning, I will note that there has been an explosion of "Jesus books" in recent years, with more on the horizon. This survey will necessarily be selective.

Bussmann, Claus. *Who Do You Say? Jesus Christ in Latin American Liberation Theology.* Maryknoll: Orbis, 1985. An excellent survey of the important contributions of liberation theologians to an interpretation of Jesus.

Borg, Marcus. *Jesus: A New Vision.* San Francisco: Harper and Row, 1987. An excellent presentation of the life and teaching of Jesus, with special attention to their social context. Very readable, it would make an ideal text.

+Borg, Marcus, and N. T. Wright. *The Meaning of Jesus: Two Visions.* San Francisco: HarperSanFranciso, 1998. Clear presentations by leading members of "third quest" for historical Jesus.

*Cook, Michael. *Jesus' Parables and the Faith That Does Justice. Studies in the Spirituality of Jesuits* 24, no. 5 (November 1992). A very interesting presentation of the importance of Jesus for the issue of justice viewed through the prism of the parables.

Crossan, J. Dominic. *The Historical Jesus: The Life of a Mediterranean Jewish Peasant*. San Francisco: Harper Collins, 1992. A massive (507 pages) reconstruction of the life of Jesus. The introductory chapters, which offer a social description of first-century society, are excellent, [Revision] as Crossan stresses very much the social implications of Jesus' teaching and actions.

+ Crossan, J. Dominic. *Jesus: A Revolutionary Biography*. San Francisco: Harper and Row, 1994. Shortened and popular version of the above.

* Chilton, Bruce, and J. H. McDonald. *Jesus and the Ethics of the Kingdom*. Grand Rapids: Eerdmans, 1987. An excellent synthetic treatment that unites the kingdom and ethics.

+ Elliott, John H. *What Is Social Scientific Criticism?* Minneapolis, Minn.: Fortress, 1993. Along with the work of Carolyn Osiek (below, p. 45), this provides a fine overview of the application of different social science models to NT study.

Furnish, Victor Paul. *The Love Command in the New Testament*. Nashville: Abingdon, 1972. An excellent coverage of all the important texts, but somewhat technical.

+ Herzog, William R., II. *Jesus, Justice and the Reign of God: A Ministry of Liberation*. Louisville: Westminster John Knox, 1999.

Horsley, Richard. *Jesus and the Spiral of Violence: Popular Resistance in Roman Palestine*. San Francisco: Harper and Row, 1987. While rejecting earlier views that Jesus was a "zealot" or even that the zealots existed during Jesus' ministry, Horsley locates Jesus' teaching among broad-based social unrest in the early first century. Chaps. 6 and 7, "Jesus and Nonviolent Social Revolution" and "The Kingdom of God and the Renewal of Israel," are both helpful.

Jeremias, Joachim. *Jerusalem in the Time of Jesus*. Minneapolis: Fortress Press, 1975. Very informative on all aspects of economic, social, and religious life in Jerusalem.

Käsemann, Ernst. "The Eschatological Royal Reign of God." In *Your Kingdom Come: Mission Perspectives*. Commission on World Mission and Evangelism. Geneva: World Council of Churches, 1981. A short but powerful essay on the social dimension of the kingdom proclamation.

* Lohfink, Gerhard. *Jesus and Community: The Social Dimension of Christian Faith*. Philadelphia: Fortress Press; New York/Ramsey: Paulist Press, 1982. Though only one half of the book is devoted to Jesus, the work is a fine statement of the social dimension of Christian faith. Like his brother, G. Lohfink argues that Christianity should be "a contrast society."

Lohfink, Norbert. "The Kingdom of God and the Economy in the Bible." *Communio* 13 (1986): 216–31. A short but very original examination of the kingdom and its background, with continued reflection on how the kingdom evokes a "contrast society."

Meier, John P. "Jesus." In the *New Jerome Biblical Commentary*, ed. R. E. Brown, J. A. Fitzmyer, and R. E. Murphy, 1320–22. Englewood Cliffs, N.J.: Prentice Hall, 1990. The best short and accurate study of Jesus.

Meier's magnum opus on Jesus comprises three volumes. The first volume, *A Marginal Jew: Rethinking the Historical Jesus* (Garden City: Doubleday, 1991), treats mainly preliminary matters for a proper reconstruction of the life and teaching of Jesus. *[Revision]* The second volume, *A Marginal Jew: Rethinking the Historical Jesus: Mentor, Message and Miracles* (Garden City: Doubleday, 1994), treats extensively of Jesus' relation to John, his kingdom proclamation, and miracles. A third and perhaps fourth volume are projected.

Mott, S. C. *Jesus and Social Ethics.* Grove Booklets on Ethics, no. 55. Malden, Mass.: Institute for Christian Renewal, 1984. An edited version of two articles that appeared in *Transformation* 1, no. 2 (April–June 1984): 21–26, and 1, No. 3 (July–Sept. 1984): 19–26; these are also published in *The Journal of Religious Ethics* 15, no. 2 (1987): 225–66, under the title "The Use of the New Testament for Social Ethics." These articles and the book present a strong criticism of the view that since Jesus founded no political system, his life and teaching cannot be invoked for systemic social-justice concerns today.

Myers, Ched. *Binding the Strong Man: A Political Reading of Mark's Story of Jesus.* Maryknoll, N.Y.: Orbis, 1988. Since I have no special treatment of Mark, I will mention this work here. It presents a powerful interpretation of Mark as written for a community engaged in passive resistance to both Roman power and the violent strategy of the Zealots.

Nolan, Albert. *Jesus before Christianity.* Maryknoll, N.Y.: Orbis, 1978. A popular and influential study of Jesus, with relevance to issues of justice and liberation.

Oakham, Douglas. *Jesus and the Economic Questions of His Day.* Toronto: Edward Mellen Press, 1986. A published dissertation, but a gold mine of information on economic life in Palestine.

+Osiek, Carolyn. *What Are They Saying about the Social Setting of the New Testament?* Rev. and enlarged, ed. New York/Rahwah, N.J.: Paulist, 1998.

Perkins, Pheme. *Love Commands in the New Testament.* New York/Ramsey: Paulist, 1982. An excellent popular treatment of all the major NT texts.

+Perkins, Pheme. "Does the New Testament Have an Economic Message?" In *Wealth in Western Thought: The Case For and Against Riches,* ed. Paul G. Schervist, 43–66. Westport, Conn.: Praeger, 1994. Other essays in this volume, though not on biblical themes are most helpful in discussion of issues of poverty and wealth.

Riches, John. *Jesus and the Transformation of Judaism.* New York: The Seabury Press, 1982. Very well informed on the social and cultural context of Jesus' teaching.

Ringe, Sharon H. *Jesus, Liberation, and the Biblical Jubilee.* Philadelphia: Fortress Press, 1985. An excellent study of the Jubilee in biblical thought and the influence of its images upon our understanding of Jesus' proclamation.

Sanders, E. P. *Jesus and Judaism,* 123–245. Philadelphia: Fortress Press, 1985. Sanders is especially sensitive to the Jewish background and context of Jesus' teaching; good on the kingdom.

Schottroff, Luise. "Non-Violence and the Love of Enemies." In R. Fuller, ed. *Essays on the Love Command,* 9–39. Philadelphia: Fortress Press, 1978. An interesting essay arguing that true love of enemies can involve actions which confront and change the enemy.

Schrage, Wolfgang. *The Ethics of the New Testament.* Philadelphia: Fortress Press, 1988. A comprehensive study synthesizing the best NT scholarship. The section on Jesus (13–106) presents an accurate exegesis of important texts, especially on the kingdom and the love command.

Song, C. S. *Jesus and the Reign of God.* Minneapolis: Fortress Press, 1993. An important study by an Asian liberation theologian.

+ Stegemann, Ekkehard W., and Woflgang Stegemann. *The Jesus Movement: A Social History of the First Century.* Minneapolis, Minn.: Fortress, 1999. One of the best discussions of the socio-economic and political context of Jesus' ministry.

+ Theissen, Gerd and A. Merz. *The Historical Jesus: A Comprehensive Guide.* Minneapolis: Fortress, 1998. A comprehensive guide to much of the recent research on Jesus and on the context of his ministry.

*Verhey, Alan. *The Great Reversal: Ethics and the New Testament.* Grand Rapids: Eerdmans, 1984. An excellent survey of NT ethics, especially pp. 1–33, on the ethics and politics of Jesus.

The Gospel of Matthew and Jewish Christianity Represented by James

My reason for joining these two works is that they reflect a similar background. Matthew, the most "Jewish" of the Gospels in its content, is written perhaps in opposition to Jewish movements at the end of the first century for the benefit of a community composed of a great number of recent converts from Judaism. Similarly, James is directed at a Jewish Christian community with a theology heavily influenced by the OT. They are also similar in emphasizing that belief and discipleship should be translated into action on behalf of powerless and poor people.

In Matthew this concern emerges in two ways. The long-recognized similarities between Jesus and Moses in Matthew would suggest that Sinai and the formation of a covenant community of responsible care for each other are a concern of Matthew. Matthew's Jesus is also concerned about faith translated into action. At the end of the Sermon on the Mount, Jesus warns against people who simply say "Lord, Lord" or who prophesy and cast out demons, but do not "bear fruit." The true disciple is the one "who listens to these words of mine and acts upon them" (7:15–24). In the scathing denunciations of the Pharisees, who may also be "Christian" Pharisees in Matthew's own community, Jesus contrasts external trappings of prestige and power with the service required of his disciples (23:1–11). The Pharisees are further castigated for stressing external observance or minutiae while neglecting the weightier things of the law, "justice, mercy, and faith" (23:23; see Hos. 2:21, where three of these are qualities of the covenant).

The section of Matthew most often invoked by a wide spectrum of Christians and non-Christians when engaged in a discussion of faith and justice is the "parable" of the Sheep and the Goats (25:31–46). Structurally, this contains the final words of Jesus before his passion and arches backward to the very beginning of the Sermon on the Mount, where suffering and persecuted people are pronounced blest by Jesus. The narrative is familiar. In a scene of apocalyptic judgment, when the Son of man will return as king and summon all the nations of the world, they will be separated like sheep and goats, the former for eternal joy, the latter for eternal punishment. The criterion for judgment will be how they treated the king (Son of Man) when he was hungry, thirsty, a stranger, naked, sick, or in prison. When both the elect and the condemned question when or how they came to the aid of the king in these circumstances, he answers, "As often as you did this to the least of my brothers and sisters, you did it to me."

The story seems simple on first reading. Jesus is identified with suffering men and women, and any who care for them with or without explicit Christological motivation gain salvation. Yet in recent years a major debate has arisen between this "universalistic" reading and a reading proposed by a number of scholars and adopted by Daniel Harrington in his new commentary on Matthew (see below, p. 49). Basing himself principally on the argument that the "little ones" in Matthew are Christian disciples and that "brother or sister" is similarly used, he interprets the parable as a judgment on pagan nations that reject the proclamation of the missionary disciples, who are to announce the teaching of Jesus "to all the nations" (28:16–20). At present there are very competent scholars on both sides, with John Meier, among others, representing the "universalistic" view.

In an article in *Theological Studies* and in *The Gospel in Parable*, I presented a modified version of the "missionary" interpretation. I felt, as well, that the "universalistic" interpretation is a bit anachronistic. Matthew is a Jewish-Christian work directed at people who believe that goodness comes from following God's word and the teaching of Jesus. The idea of the "anonymous Christian" behind the "universalistic" interpretation would be foreign to Matthew. Basically, I argued that sufferings such as hunger, thirst, imprisonment, nakedness, and weakness are the very kinds of things Paul mentions as the lot of the missionary (1 Cor. 4:9–13; 2 Cor. 4:8f., 6:4f., 11:23–29). In an apocalyptic context, however, the key point is that the people who assist the hungry and other sufferers are called "just." Treatment of the least, who I argued are Christians in mission and witnesses to the world, becomes the occasion by which the true meaning of justice is revealed. What is done positively *for them* is not to be limited *to them*. The Christian disciple, through a life of witness and even martyrdom, is the occasion by which eschatological justice is made visible to the world. Like Jesus, the disciples in mission are to be the occasion of the disclosure of God's will for all peoples. This interpretation (a bit over-condensed here) would, I felt, maintain the stress on the doing of justice characteristic of the universalistic interpretation, while avoiding the sectarian overtones of the missionary interpretation. It also makes the Church the primary recipient of the challenge of the Gospel. Only a Church in mission bearing apostolic sufferings will provide the witness necessary for God's justice to be revealed in the world.

The Jewish-Christian Letter of James presents a severe and pragmatic spirituality. One of its early exhortations is "Be doers of the word and not hearers only, deluding yourselves" (1:22), which is followed by the definition of true religion as "to care for orphans and widows in their affliction and to keep oneself unstained by the world" (1:27). James exhorts his community to avoid partiality and in biting language mocks the attention given to the rich and powerful, even though the rich are oppressing the community (2:1–7). He criticizes his listeners for dishonoring a poor person, even though God chose the poor to become heirs of the kingdom. In line with being doers as well as hearers of the word, James declares that faith without works is dead and specifies one of the works as clothing and feeding a poor brother or sister (2:14–17). Towards the end of the letter, James voices one of the NT's most violent denunciations of the rich: "Come now, you rich, weep and wail over your impending miseries." In addition to amassing gold and silver jewelry, the rich have withheld the wages of their harvesters and lived on earth in luxury and pleasure—"you have fattened your hearts for the day of slaughter" (5:1–6). Behind the words of James can be heard Amos of Tekoa almost seven centuries earlier.

Bibliography on Matthew and James

Balch, David, ed. *Social History of the Matthean Community: Cross Disciplinary Approaches.* Minneapolis: Fortress Press, 1991. A collection of scholarly articles that offer descriptions of the social context of Matthew.

Cope, Lamar. "Matthew XXV: 31–46, 'The Sheep and the Goats,' Reinterpreted." *Novum Testamentum* 11 (1969): 32–44. This is the most succinct statement of the "missionary" interpretation of Matthew 25:31–46.

Crosby, Michael. *House of Disciples: Church, Economics and Justice in Matthew.* Maryknoll: Orbis, 1988. Using "house" as a root metaphor, Crosby derives a vision of social justice from Matthew. The work is a bit sprawling, with a somewhat undigested mixture of methods, and thus is not easy to read.

Donahue, John R. "The 'Parable' of the Sheep and the Goats: A Challenge to Christian Ethics." *Theological Studies* 47 (1986): 3–31. A somewhat shortened version of this is in Donahue, *The Gospel in Parable: Metaphor, Narrative and Theology in the Synoptic Gospels,* 109–25. Philadelphia: Fortress Press, 1988.

Garland, David. *The Intention of Matthew 23.* Novum Testamentum Supplementum, no. 52. Leiden: E. J. Brill, 1979. An important study showing that much of the anti-Pharisaic material of Matt. 23 is directed at Christian "Pharisaism."

Harrington, Daniel. *The Gospel of Matthew.* Sacra Pagina, no. 1. Collegeville: Liturgical Press, 1991. An excellent commentary at the level of "religious professional" in what promises to be an important series.

Johnson, Luke T. "The Use of Leviticus in James." *Journal of Biblical Literature* 101 (1982): 391–401. It traces the influence on James of the social legislation of Leviticus.

Maynard-Reid, Pedrito U. *Poverty and Wealth in James.* Maryknoll: Orbis, 1987. A well-researched and interesting study of the pertinent section of James, with attention to the background and social setting.

*Meier, J. *Matthew.* New Testament Message, no. 3. Wilmington: Glazier, 1980. The most insightful commentary on Matthew in English.

Overmann, J. A. *Matthew's Gospel and Formative Judaism: The Social World of the Matthean Community.* Minneapolis: Fortress Press, 1990. A very interesting study of Matthew in relation to the different forms of Judaism in the first century. Important for evaluating "anti-Jewish" statements in Matthew.

Schweizer, Eduard. *The Good News according to Matthew.* Atlanta: John Knox, 1975. An excellent commentary with theological sensitivity.

Shepherd, Massey. "The Epistle of James and the Gospel of Matthew." *Journal of Biblical Literature* 75 (1956): 40–51.

Smith, R. H. *Matthew.* Minneapolis: Augsburg, 1989. An excellent popular commentary.

Tamez, Elsa. *The Scandalous Message of James.* New York: Crossroad, 1990. A fresh and powerful reading "from the perspective of the oppressed."

Viviano, Benjamin. "The Gospel according to Matthew." In the *New Jerome Biblical Commentary,* 630–74.

+Wainwright, Elaine. *Shall We Look for Another? A Feminist Reading of the Matthean Jesus.* Maryknoll, N.Y.: Orbis, 1998.

The Gospel of Luke and the Acts of the Apostles

The Lucan writings constitute about one quarter of the whole NT. With the exception of James, these writings contain the most explicit statements on wealth, poverty, and the use of resources. Luke's special concern is manifest from his editing of the Marcan tradition and, most importantly, by the incorporation of "L" material (=material found only in Luke), which is itself a combination of tradition and Lucan composition. Luke-Acts has also been that NT work most often invoked on issues of social justice and concern for the marginal.

The Gospel of Luke

1. The infancy narratives show a special concern for the 'ānāwîm (people without money and power). In her "Magnificat" Mary praises a God who puts down the mighty from their thrones, fills the hungry with good things, and sends the rich away empty (Luke 1:52f.). The first proclamation of Jesus' birth is to people on the margin of society ("shepherds" [2:8–14]); the sacrifice offered at the presentation is that determined by law for poor people (2:24); Simeon and Anna (a widow) represent faithful and just people (2:25–38).

2. To the Q tradition about John's preaching, Luke adds an exhortation that the one who has two coats should share with the one who has none (3:10).

3. Luke begins the public ministry of Jesus, not with the proclamation of the imminence of the kingdom (compare with Mark 1:15 and Matt. 4:17), but with Jesus citing Isa. 61:1–2: "the good news to the poor" (Luke 4:17–19; see also 7:22).

4. Only in Luke does Levi "leave everything" when he follows Jesus (5:28; compare with Mark 2:14 and Matt. 9:9).

5. In Luke it is simply "the poor" who are blessed, and Luke adds woes against the rich and powerful (6:20, 24–26). Luke adds these words to the saying on forgiveness: "Give and it will be given to you" (6:38).

6. Only Luke contains the parables of the Rich Fool (12:13–21), of the Unjust Steward (16:1–8), and of the Rich Man and Lazarus (16:19–31).

7. Only in Luke is the "great banquet" to be celebrated with "the poor, the maimed, the lame, and the blind" (14:13, 21).

8. Only Luke recounts the story of Zaccheus, the "chief tax collector," who upon his conversion is willing to give half his goods to the poor (19:8).

9. Luke presents Jesus in the form of an OT prophet who takes the side of the widow (7:11–17, 18:1–8), the stranger in the land (10:25–37, 17:16), and those on the margin of society (14:12f., 21).

Rich and Poor in the Acts of the Apostles

1. In Luke's version of the death of Judas (Acts 1:18–20), in contrast to Matt. 27:3–10, Judas does not return the money, but "buys a farm" (see 4:32) with the "payment of his injustice"; he seems to die accidentally and the farm is deserted (cursed).

2. The early community is one that shares its goods in common; in it there is no needy person (2:41–47, 4:32–37).

3. In both the Gospel and Acts, almsgiving is stressed (Luke 11:41, 12:33, 19:8; Acts 10:2, 4, 31; 24:17).

4. Ananias and Sapphira (Acts 5:1–11), by withholding the "proceeds of the land," are guilty of deceiving God. Though they were free to give or not to give the proceeds, their possessions became an occasion for duplicity.

5. Simon tries to use money (v. 18) to buy power (8:9–24).

6. Lydia, "the seller of purple" who was a worshiper of God, shows Paul hospitality, thus giving an example of the good use of resources (16:11–15); see also 17:12, where upper-class men and women accept the Gospel.

7. Paul and Silas are beaten for freeing a slave girl from venal owners (16:16–24); see also 19:23–41, where the silversmiths of Ephesus feel their livelihood threatened by Paul's preaching.

8. Paul concludes his final address to the Ephesians with comments about the use of goods and concern for the poor (20:32–35).

From this overview it is clear that the Lucan writings present a dilemma. In the Gospel, riches are evil when they become such a preoccupation that they dominate a person's whole life or when a person attempts to secure the future through them, as in the case of the rich fool. They are also evil, as in the parable of Dives and Lazarus, when they blind people to the suffering neighbor at their doorstep. Discipleship demands renunciation of one's goods and adoption of the itinerant lifestyle of Jesus. Acts does not develop the more radical statements of the Gospel. Here the proper use of possessions through mutual sharing and almsgiving, rather than total dispossession, is commended. As Luke Johnson notes, if hospitality to the missionary was such an important aspect of Acts (and Paul), there must have been a great number of Christians who retained their homes and resources. If almsgiving is praised, the community could not have been composed of the wandering dispossessed.

Many solutions (see Donahue, "Two Decades") have been proposed for this dilemma, ranging from the older view of a two-level morality—one for the committed disciple and one for the ordinary Christian—to views that Luke accurately portrays the difference between the teaching of the earthly Jesus and its accommodation in the ongoing life of a first-century Church. In the latter case, the teaching of Jesus is only of historical interest and possesses no lasting value as a model or ideal for subsequent Christians.

I would suggest (somewhat tentatively) that the social setting of the final composition of Luke-Acts offers guidelines for interpretation. Luke-Acts was put together most likely in a Hellenistic city between A.D. 85–95. At this time more and more people of comparatively more abundant means and higher social status were entering the Church. As I noted earlier, economic difference in antiquity was accompanied by social discrimination and often scorn for "the lower classes." By stressing the radical poverty of Jesus and his first followers and by emphasizing their origins among people of low status, Luke reminds his community of their "roots." Though Jesus can be acclaimed as "Lord and Savior," titles normally reserved to the Roman emperor, he himself was of low status and died a criminal's death. His followers lived as a community without status and class division. At the same time, in the Jewish tradition of almsgiving ("For almsgiving delivers from death and keeps you from entering the darkness" [Tob. 4:10]), Luke exhorts his community to a proper use of wealth by putting it at the service of others. The old Deuteronomic ideal of a community where there are no needy persons has been resurrected by Luke (Deut. 15:4, Acts 4:34).

Bibliography on Luke–Acts

Cassidy, Richard J. *Jesus, Politics and Society: A Study of Luke's Gospel.* Maryknoll, N.Y.: Orbis, 1978.

———. *Society and Politics in the Acts of the Apostles.* Maryknoll, N.Y.: Orbis, 1988. Cassidy's two works are important contributions to understanding the social status and political perspectives of Luke's community. The author rejects a view that Luke portrays Roman power in a favorable light.

Donahue, John R. *The Gospel in Parable* (p. 49 above), 162–80, on Luke's parables dealing with the poor.

———. "Two Decades of Research on the Rich and the Poor in Luke-Acts." In D. A. Knight and P. J. Paris, eds. *Justice and the Holy: Essays in Honor of Walter Harrelson,* 129–44. Atlanta, Ga.: Scholars Press, 1989.

Dupont, J. *Les Beatitudes.* 3 vols. Paris: Gabalda, 1969, 1973. See especially 2:19–142; 3:41–64, 151–206, 389–471. A classic study that had immense impact on interpreting the beatitudes as not simply promises of future bliss.

———. The Poor and Poverty in the Gospels." *Gospel Poverty.* Ed. A. George, 25–52. Chicago: Franciscan Herald, 1971.

———. "Community of Goods in the Early Church." In *The Salvation of the Gentiles: Studies in the Acts of the Apostles,* 85–102. New York: Paulist, 1979.

D'Sa, Thomas. "The Salvation of the Rich in the Gospel of Luke." *Vidyajoti* 52 (1988): 170–80.

*Esler, Philip. F. *Community and Gospel in Luke-Acts: The Social and Political Motivations of Lucan Theology.* Society for New Testament Studies Monograph Series, no. 57. Cambridge: Cambridge University, 1987. Very interesting and informative. Chap. 7, "The Poor and the Rich," presents excellent material on what it was to be "poor" in the Hellenistic world and locates Luke in this context.

Fitzmyer, J. A. *The Gospel according to Luke, I–IX,* and *The Gospel according to Luke, X–XXIV.* Anchor Bible, nos. 28 and 28A. Garden City, N.Y.: Doubleday and Co., 1981, 1985. Probably the best commentary on Luke in any language. The introductory essay in *Luke, I–IX,* "A Sketch of Lukan Theology" (143–270), is the finest synthesis available of Luke's theology.

Gillman, John. *Possessions and the Life of Faith: A Reading of Luke-Acts.* Zaccheus Studies. Collegeville: Liturgical Press, 1991. A very good popular presentation covering major texts and areas.

Hamel, Gildas. *Poverty and Charity in Roman Palestine, First Three Centuries C.E.* Berkeley: University of California Press, 1990. Though this is not on Luke, I have listed it here because it is a magnificent study of poverty and the attempts to alleviate it, based on evidence in Jewish, Greco-Roman, and Christian sources.

Johnson, Luke T. *The Literary Function of Possessions in Luke-Acts.* Society of Biblical Literature Dissertation Series, no. 39. Missoula, Mont.: Scholars, 1977.

Karris, Robert J. "Poor and Rich: The Lukan *Sitz im Leben."* In *Perspectives on Luke-Acts,* ed. C. H. Talbert, 112–25. Danville, Va.: Association of Baptist Professors of Religion, 1978.

Keck, L. E. "The Poor among the Saints in the New Testament." *Zeitschrift für Neutestamentliche Wissenschaft* 56 (1965): 100–129.

———. "The Poor among the Saints in Jewish Christianity and Qumran." *Zeitschrift für Neutestamentliche Wissenschaft* 57 (1966): 54–78. Keck's two articles offer a fine scholarly overview of important texts and background material.

Navone, J. *Themes of St. Luke.* Rome: Gregorian University, 1970. Available from Loyola University Press, Chicago, Ill. An excellent catalog of Lucan themes.

Pilgrim, Walter E. *Good News to the Poor: Wealth and Poverty in Luke-Acts.* Minneapolis: Augsburg, 1981. Probably the best overview of the Lucan writings, with fine sections on the OT background.

Schmidt, T. E. *Hostility to Wealth in the Synoptic Gospels.* Sheffield: Journal for the Study of the Old Testament Press, 1987. Covering more than Luke, this is technical but comprehensive.

Stegemann, Wolfgang. *The Gospel and the Poor.* Philadelphia: Fortress Press, 1984. An excellent short study which covers more than Luke. One of the best works to use in a pastoral setting.

———. "The Following of Christ as Solidarity between Rich, Respected Christians and Poor, Despised Christians (Gospel of Luke)." In L. Schottroff and W. Stegemann. *Jesus and the Hope of the Poor,* 67–120. Maryknoll, N.Y.: Orbis 1986.

Pauline Theology and the Issues of Faith and Justice

A certain paradox confronts us when we approach Paul. On the one hand, no NT author uses the term *dikaiosynē* (justice) more than Paul, nor does any other author link it so explicitly with issues of faith. Yet the contemporary concern for social justice has been most often based on OT considerations (Exodus, the Prophetic concern for the poor) or on the teaching of Jesus. Three principal reasons explain the neglect of Paul:

1. The traditional theological debate over "faith and works" and justification by faith has given a radical individualistic bent to presentations of Pauline theology, often phrased in terms of how the individual sinner finds acceptance by God.

2. Since Paul is the most "theological" of the NT writers, it is those portions of his letters that receive prime attention. The later sections of

most letters, where Paul deals with practical problems facing the communities, are rushed through, and their relation to the theological sections is not developed.

3. Since Albert Schweitzer, Paul has been accused of teaching only an "interim ethic." Evidence for this would be in his exhortation to people not to change their marital or social status because "the time is short." Paul's eschatological view that the shape of the world is passing away and his own personal hope to be with the Lord have made some interpreters doubt whether Paul's ethics offers any help for Christians settling in for the long haul of history.

I would like to offer some suggestions on how both Paul's theology and his pastoral engagement in the lives of his communities provide resources for the faith that does justice.

Theological Observations

Central to Paul's thought is the proclamation of the Christ event, which Joseph A. Fitzmyer has described as "the meaning that the person and lordship of Jesus of Nazareth had and still has for human history and existence." ("Pauline Theology," *New Jerome Biblical Commentary*, 1389). It is equivalent to the "objective redemption" and embraces "the complex of decisive moments of the earthly and risen life of Jesus Christ"—specifically, his passion, death, and resurrection, along with his burial, exaltation, and heavenly intercession (ibid., 1397). This "Christ event" as proclaimed and lived by Paul has a number of implications for issues of social justice.

1. **The Christ event as the foundation of Christian Faith demands responsibility for the world.** Christian faith in the death and resurrection is not simply faith in the promise of eternal life, but faith in the *victory over death* achieved in Jesus. Through baptism, Christians participate *already* in this victory: "We were buried therefore with him by baptism into death, so that as Christ was raised from the dead by the glory of the Father, we too might walk *in the newness of life*" (Rom. 6:4). Here in Romans Paul does *not* say, as does the author of Colossians, that the Christian has risen with Christ. The resurrection has an ethical counterpart, "walking in the newness of life." Also, in Paul the Christian contrast is *not* between earth and heaven or between material and spiritual reality, but between the "old age" and "the new" (see especially Rom. 8, 2 Cor. 5:16–21). Fundamental to new life in Christ is the experience of "power" ("With great power the Apostles gave testimony to the resurrection of the Lord Jesus" [Acts 4:32–37; see also 1 Cor. 1:18–31, 2 Cor. 12:9–13]). The Christian is to be a *witness in mission* of the victory

over death and the transforming power of the resurrection. To pursue the quest for justice in faith means that the Christian walks in confidence that evil is not the Lord of life and that even death for the sake of others cannot separate a person from the love of God (Rom. 8:28–39).

2. **Justification of the sinner by God's grace through faith results in a personal and communal liberation that enables people to live for others rather than for themselves.** Theologically, Paul states that the Christ event frees the Christian from sin, law, and death. Equally important as this "freedom from" is the Pauline notion of "freedom for." Paul stated this succinctly: "For freedom Christ has set us free" (Gal. 5:1a). Freedom for Paul is liberation from the self-serving and self-destructive aspects of "striving for" and "boasting of" human achievements, in order to direct one's attention to the needs of others. In Galatians, which along with Romans is his major theological statement on justification, after having somewhat polemically rejected those opponents who want to reimpose Jewish practices on Gentile Christians, Paul says: "For you were called for freedom, brothers and sisters. But do not use this freedom as an opportunity for self indulgence ['flesh'], but through love become servants of one another" (Gal. 5:13). Paul then goes on to describe "walking according to the spirit" and "walking according to the flesh" (5:16–21). The virtues and vices listed here for the most part either foster or destroy life in community. Paul then concludes this whole section with the statement: "Bear one another's burdens, and so you will fulfill the law of Christ" (6:2).

Therefore, the justified and graced Christian is a person who does not seek a community of isolated individuals, but rather one in which concern for the weak and suffering is the touchstone of living according to the law of Christ. The final sentences of the United States bishops' letter on economic justice capture this aspect of Paul's thought:

> We know that we are called to be members of a new covenant of love. We have to move from our devotion to independence through an understanding of interdependence, to a commitment to human solidarity. That challenge must find its realization in the kind of community we build among us. Love implies concern for all—especially the poor—and a continued search for those social and economic structures that permit everyone to share in a community that is a part of redeemed creation (Rom. 8:21–23).

3. **Pauline eschatology does not warrant an "interim ethic," but rather summons Christians to responsibility for life in the world.** Since Albert Schweitzer's challenge that Paul provided only an "interim ethic," significant research has been done on the social context and meaning of Paul's eschatology. For Paul, the Christian lives between the "already"

and the "not yet." Through Christ the evil powers have been subdued (Phil. 2:10f.) and Christians live in the new age (1 Cor. 10:11, 2 Cor. 5:17). Yet Paul has an eschatological reservation. All creation is groaning (Rom. 8:23) and Christians are to look forward to the final victory over death, when the risen Christ hands over the kingdom to his Father (1 Cor. 15:51–54). Between the "already" and the "not yet," Christians are to walk in the newness of life and not let sin reign in their mortal bodies (Rom. 6:12). They should yield themselves to God, so that they might become instruments and servants of justice (Rom. 6:13, 18). Eschatology thus provides a "view from the end," a vision of a restored creation and of the kind of community that should exist in the world, and summons Christians to implement this vision, however incomplete, in their individual and social lives.

Paul's Practical and Pastoral Directives

Paul is not simply an itinerant missionary moving feverishly from one city to another, but a pastor deeply concerned with life in his communities. Some of these concerns have bearing on issues of faith and justice today.

Principal among these is Paul's concern to collect money for the churches in Judea. For approximately eight years, from the Jerusalem Council (approximately A.D. 48–49; see also Gal. 2:10) until the letter to the Romans (about 56–57; see Rom. 15:25–29), Paul manifests concern for the collection. Much of his work among the Corinthians is taken up with the collection (1 Cor. 16:1–4, 2 Cor. 8f.). For Paul the collection is not simply an act of charity, but a way to affirm solidarity between the Greek churches and the Jerusalem mother church. Such a view is significant today. The growing gap between rich and poor within Catholics in the United States is not simply an economic problem, but a problem of the unity of faith within the body of Christ. As U.S. Catholics move up the economic ladder, they often forget their immigrant and working-class origins. Effective concern for the growing number of Latino Catholics and the new immigrants from Asia, many of whom are Catholic, is a way to affirm the inclusive vision permeating Paul's writings.

Also a reading of 2 Cor. 8f. shows that Paul envisages a relation between rich and poor that avoids heavy-handed moralism in dealing with the more prosperous and respects the dignity of the poor, rather than treating them as "objects of charity." Following to some degree the later Jesuit pedagogical principle of *emulatio*, he tells the Corinthians about the generosity of the economically less-well-off Macedonian churches (Thessalonica and Philippi), with a hint that they can do likewise. After invoking the example of Christ, who "though rich became poor for your sake," he tells the Corinthians that, "as a matter of equality, your abundance should supply their want, so that their abundance may supply your want." Paul goes on to explain that the spiritual abundance of the Jerusalem church will be a reciprocal gift for the material abundance of the Corinthian communities. He will also argue that any gift should be freely given from a motive of generosity, "for God loves a cheerful giver." The important thing is not that we try to translate Paul's collection rhetoric and strategy into present-day practice, but that he provides an example of theological ideas translated into concrete action for the poor.

The second issue is the dispute over the celebration of the Lord's Supper. At Corinth the Eucharist was celebrated in the context of an ordinary meal, when Christians gathered in the evening at the end of the customary working day. The only place with enough space for a community gathering would normally have been the home of one of the more prosperous members of the community.

Paul directly addresses problems with the Supper. "I heard that when you meet as a community [as a church], there are divisions among you"; then he gives his initial judgment on the situation: "When you meet in one place, then, **it is not the Lord's supper that you are eating,** for when the time comes to eat, each one goes ahead with his own supper and one goes hungry, while another gets drunk" (1 Cor. 11:22f.).

Thanks principally to the work of Gerd Theissen, we are able to see that this theological quarrel had a social and ethical dimension. Apparently, the more prosperous members of the community simply became hungry and tired of waiting for the small artisans and day laborers to arrive after a working day that stretched from dawn to dusk. They began the celebration of the Lord's Supper and also ate special food and drink that they had prepared for themselves rather than sharing it with others. Paul reacts strongly to this practice: "Do you not have houses in which you can eat or drink?" (1 Cor. 11f.); then he proceeds to highlight the evil effect of this custom: "Do you show contempt for the church of God, and humiliate those who have nothing?" (the Greek here is literally "the have-nots"). Paul is in effect saying that those social distinctions between upper-class and lower-class people that are part of the fabric of the Hellenistic world have no place in the Christian assembly. One might recall here Paul's early statement to the Galatians that in Christ there is neither Jew nor Greek, slave nor free, male nor female (Gal. 3:26).

After this initial programmatic assault on the position of those who were shaming the have-nots, Paul cites the tradition of the institution of the Eucharist, which is parallel to accounts found in the Synoptic Gospels and very similar to the words of institution used at Mass today. Having evoked this tradition, Paul then applies it to the situation in the community. He first says that anyone who eats the bread or drinks the cup of the Lord unworthily will have to answer for the body and blood of the Lord (11:27), and that anyone who eats and drinks without discerning the body eats and drinks judgment on himself (11:28). I will unpack these statements a bit.

For Paul the words of institution make present again the self-offering of Christ: "My body for you." The "you" are all the Christians equally. As Paul has noted in other places, Jesus died like one who did not choose his own benefit but that of others, dying for the weak or marginal Christian brother or sister as well as for the powerful. "For none of us lives to himself alone and none of us dies to himself alone" (Rom. 14:7) expresses for Paul the real meaning of imitation of Christ. The practices of the Corinthians are a direct affront to the example of Christ. By preferring their own good and shaming other community members of lower social and economic status, they are making a mockery of the Eucharist. This explains Paul's harsh judgment: "It is not the Lord's supper that you are eating."

When Paul says that one who eats **without discerning the body** eats and drinks judgment on oneself (11:28), the "body" is a reference not primarily to the body of Jesus (as the later concept of sacrilege affirmed), but the community as the body of Christ (which he will discuss in great detail in the following chapter). Discerning the body for Paul means assessing the impact of one's actions on the good of the community, especially in regard to its weaker members, and asking how the actions of the community re-present Christ in the world.

Paul's directives here show that issues of justice and concern for the more vulnerable members of the community enter into the most central act of Christian community, the celebration of the Lord's Supper. They also show Paul's constant concern for the weaker members of the community and for the creation of a community in which economic and social divisions do not invalidate the faith that the community as a whole professes. Contemporary Christians are faced with the challenge to join together worship and social action, to live in such a fashion that there is no gap between the faith they celebrate on Sunday and the way they live the other six days of the week. (See also the bibliography on liturgy and social justice.)

Bibliography on Paul

The potential bibliography is vast. I will select works that present leading Pauline theological motifs and those bearing on his ethics. For an excellent overview of all aspects of Paul, see J. A. Fitzmyer, "Paul," *New Jerome Biblical Commentary,* 1329–37, and "Pauline Theology, ibid., 1382–1416; this is also available as *Paul and His Theology: A Brief Sketch.* 2nd ed. (Englewood Cliffs, N.J.: Prentice Hall, 1987).

*Bassler, Jouette. *God and Mammon: Asking for Money in the New Testament.* Nashville: Abingdon Press, 1991. A popular and learned presentation with stress on Paul.

Beker, J. Christian. *Paul the Apostle: The Triumph of God in Life and Thought.* Philadelphia: Fortress Press 1980. A major theological study focusing on the apocalyptic in Paul.

———. *Paul's Apocalyptic Gospel: The Coming Triumph of God.* Philadelphia: Fortress Press, 1982. A popular and much-condensed presentation of major ideas contained in the above work.

Betz, Hans Dieter. *2 Corinthians 8–9.* Hermeneia. Philadelphia: Fortress Press 1986. A technical but informative treatment of the "collection" letters.

+Elliott, Neil. *Liberating Paul: The Justice of God and the Politics of the Apostle.* Maryknoll, N.Y.: Orbis, 1994. Challenges interpretations of justice in Paul that seem to ignore social dimension of Paul. See also his "Romans 13:1–7 in the Context of Imperial Propaganda," in Horsely, *Paul and Empire.*

Furnish, Victor P. *Theology and Ethics in Paul.* Nashville: Abingdon Press, 1968. An older but thorough work.

*———. *The Moral Teaching of Paul: Selected Issues.* Nashville: Abingdon, 1979. Excellent short studies on issues of marriage, divorce, homosexuality, and church and state.

Georgi, Dieter. *Remembering the Poor: The History of Paul's Collection for Jerusalem.* Nashville: Abingdon Press, 1992. A translation of Georgi's important 1965 scholarly study of the collection.

Hock, Ronald. *The Social Context of Paul's Ministry.* Philadelphia: Fortress Press, 1980. A good short picture of Paul's trade (leather worker) and its implication for his theology.

+Horsley, Richard A., ed. *Paul and Empire: Religion and Power in Imperial Society.* Harrisburg, Pa.: Trinity Press International, 1997. Good collection of essays on social and cultural context of Paul that sheds light on certain "revolutionary" aspects of his thought.

*Murphy-O'Connor, Jerome. *Becoming Human Together: The Pastoral Anthropology of St. Paul.* Good News Studies. Wilmington, Del.: Michael Glazier, 1982. An original and very interesting presentation; see especially parts 2 and 3, "Society" and "Community."

————. "Eucharist and Community in 1 Corinthians." *Worship* 50 (1976): 370 –85; 51 (1977): 56–69. Interesting and important essays.

Nickle, Keith. *The Collection: A Study of Paul's Strategy.* Studies in Biblical Theology, no. 48. Naperville: Allenson, 1966. A somewhat technical but thorough study.

Schrage, Wolfgang, see p. 46 above, especially chap. 4.

+Tamez, Elsa. *The Amnesty of Grace: Justification by Faith from a Latin American Perspective.* Nashville: Abingdon, 1993. Latin American non-Catholic scholar relates teaching on justification to social concerns.

*Theissen, Gerd. *The Social Setting of Pauline Christianity: Essays on Corinth.* Philadelphia: Fortress Press, 1982. Important studies of the social context of Paul; see especially chap. 4, "Social Integration and Sacramental Activity: An Analysis of 1 Corinthians 11:17–34."

Tobin, Thomas. *The Spirituality of Paul.* Message of Biblical Spirituality. Wilmington, Del.: Michael Glazier, 1986. A synthetic and readable overview of Paul.

The Book of Revelation

Because of its "otherwordly" character, its sanguinary hope of divine vengeance on enemies, and its use by fundamentalist groups, Revelation (The Apocalypse) often seems of little use for reflection on the Bible and social justice. Yet, as Adella Yarbro Collins notes, this work reminds us that the love command of Jesus must be complemented by the call for justice found in the Apocalypse (*The Apocalypse,* p. x). Apocalyptic literature in the OT, in the intertestamental literature, and in the NT arises from a consciousness that the world is "out of joint." It originates most often from marginal or persecuted groups, and its vivid imagery conveys a hope for divine vindication. Though employing vivid images of battle and warfare, Revelation describes a struggle to be fought by divine power, since the human struggle reflects a heavenly battle between God and cosmic forces opposed to God. Paradoxically, apocalyptic literature diffuses the human desire for vengeance and assures those persecuted that God is ultimately on their side and that evil will not triumph in the end. It can provide a powerful warrant for nonviolent resistance to massive social evil and sustain communities with the hope of God's presence.

▶ ◀

Bibliography on Apocalyptic and Revelation

Barr, David. L. "The Apocalypse as a Symbolic Transformation of the World." *Interpretation* 38 (1984): 39–50.

*Collins, Adela Yarbro. *The Apocalypse*. New Testament Message, no. 22. Wilmington, Del.: Michael Glazier, 1979. One of the most helpful popular commentaries on the Apocalypse by an expert on apocalyptic literature.

―――. "Reading the Book of Revelation in the Twentieth Century." *Interpretation* 40 (July 1986): 229–42. A fine survey of contemporary approaches to apocalyptic. Other articles in this issue are also most helpful.

Collins, John J. *The Apocalyptic Imagination: An Introduction to the Jewish Matrix of Christianity*. New York: Crossroad, 1984. The best introduction to those texts classed as apocalyptic.

Jewett, Robert. "Coming to Terms with the Boom Doom." *Quarterly Review* 4 (1984): 9–22. Good guidelines for interpreting apocalyptic.

Schüssler Fiorenza, Elisabeth. *The Book of Revelation: Justice and Judgment*. Philadelphia: Fortress Press, 1985. An excellent collection of essays; see especially chap. 7, "Visionary Rhetoric and Socio-Political Situation."

―――. *Revelation: Vision of a Just World*. Minneapolis: Fortress Press, 1991. An excellent introduction, followed by a section-by-section commentary.

APPLICATION AND INTERPRETATION
OF BIBLICAL MATERIAL

M y purpose thus far has been to highlight biblical themes, blocks of literature, and secondary resources that provide reflection on the faith that does justice. Most Jesuits will use this material principally in some ministry of the word—preaching, teaching, retreats, or spiritual direction. I would like now to offer some admittedly inadequate guidelines for use of this material, as well as bibliographical resources. I will also add bibliography on feminist hermeneutics and the relation of peace and justice, since these are important issues related to the quest for justice in the Bible.

Often more important than the preparation of the sermon or the class is the preparation of the preacher or the teacher. The first task is to gain an increased knowledge of pertinent biblical texts in their historical and literary context and to read them with a concern for issues of social justice. Allied to this is a "hermeneutics of suspicion" about interpretations supporting individualized piety. Philip Esler (p. 53 above) states that Luke's writings are read through a layer of *embourgeoisment* to foster middle-class values. One way to avoid this is to become aware of the social dimension and the social context of biblical material.

Second, though virtually no one feels that the Bible offers concrete directives or solutions to today's complex social problems, the Bible is the foundation of a Judeo-Christian vision of life. It discloses the kind of God we love and worship. This God is interested in the world, in human history, and in the manner in which humans live in community. This interest is pervasive throughout both testaments. In one sense, the "faith that does justice" is simply an application of the great command to love God with one's whole heart, mind, and soul and the neighbor as oneself. What the Bible relentlessly affirms, from the law of Moses to the Pauline summons "to bear another's burdens and so fulfill the law of Christ" (Gal. 6:2), is that the love of neighbor is manifest especially in care for the weak and the powerless.

Third, often the best way to speak about the inner meaning of justice as understood in the Bible, is often not explicitly to talk about justice, but about *what justice means and about its related terms*, for example, treating people with dignity; awareness of God's love for the "outsider"; fidelity to the demands of relationships on one's life; loving kindness, compassion (often read Hos. 2:19–21). Get in touch with the parables and stories of Jesus where the fundamental meanings of justice are affirmed, for example, the Good Samaritan, the Rich Man and Lazarus.

Fourth, some principle of analogy is helpful for application of the biblical texts. Though the social and cultural situation of biblical texts is very different from our modern, postindustrial society, there are profound similarities, especially at the level of human behavior. Amos's criticism of the ostentatious rich (2:6f., 4:1, 6:4–7), the plight of the poor man in Ps. 10, and the blindness of the wealthy to the needy at their gates (Luke 16:19–31) are hauntingly familiar in our own day. Paul's concern for the poorer churches of Palestine and even his collection strategy has relevance to a church in the United States increasingly divided along socioeconomic lines. Paul Tillich once defined the task of theology as one of correlating the symbols of the faith (where symbol is understood as sacred text and sacred tradition) with the existential question of a given age. In our age socioeconomic questions are the most pressing; and conversion, study, and imagination are necessary to achieve the task of correlation.

▶   ◀

Bibliography on the Use of Scripture for Ethics

*Bauckham, R. *The Bible in Politics: How to Read the Bible Politically*. Third Way Books. London: S.P.C.K., 1989. An introduction to hermeneutical problems and a discussion of significant texts by a well-respected British NT scholar.

Barr, James. "The Bible as a Political Document." *Bulletin of the John Rylands Library* 62 (1980): 268–98. Important observations by a well-respected biblical scholar, with certain cautions about the use of the Bible for social ethics.

Birch, Bruce C., and Larry Rasmussen. *The Bible and Ethics in Christian Life.* Rev. ed. Minneapolis: Augsburg, 1989. The best single resource.

Cahill, Lisa Sowle. "The New Testament and Ethics: Communities of Social Change." *Interpretation* 44 (1990): 383–95.

Collins, R. F. *Christian Morality: Biblical Foundations.* Notre Dame: University of Notre Dame Press, 1986.

Curran, Charles E. "The Role and Function of the Scriptures in Moral Theology." In C. Curran and R. McCormick, eds. *The Use of Scripture in Moral Theology.* Readings in Moral Theology, no. 4. New York/Ramsey, N.J.: Paulist, 1984. All the essays in this volume are most helpful, especially the following ones by J. Gustafson.

Gustafson, James M. "The Changing Use of the Bible in Christian Ethics." In *The Use of Scripture in Moral Theology,* 133–51. Readings in Moral Theology, no. 4. New York/Ramsey, N.J.: Paulist, 1984.

———. "The Place of Scripture in Christian Ethics: A Methodological Study." In *The Use of Scripture in Moral Theology,* 151–78. Readings in Moral Theology, no. 4. New York/Ramsey, N.J.: Paulist, 1984.

Hays, R. B. "Scripture-Shaped Community: The Problem of Method in New Testament Ethics." *Interpretation* 44 (1990): 42–55. *New Testament Abstracts* 34.847.

Himes, K. R. "Scripture and Ethics: A Review Essay." *Biblical Theology Bulletin* 15 (1985): 65–73.

Kysar, R. *Called to Care: Biblical Images for Social Ministry.* Minneapolis, Minn.: Fortress Press, 1991. A short and readable survey of biblical images of God and their relation to social ministry, with pastoral reflections on challenges to social ministry, for example, changing consciousness and overcoming fear.

Sandeen, Ernest, ed. *The Bible and Social Reform.* Chico, Cal.: Scholars Press, 1982. A study of how the Bible has been used by North American theologians concerned with social issues.

*Schneiders, Sandra M. *The Revelatory Text: Interpreting the New Testament as Sacred Scripture.* San Francisco: Harper Collins, 1991. Though not explicitly on the use of Scripture for issues of justice, this work provides the best discussion of how to bridge the gap between academic study of the Bible and its use in the Church. Though dealing with complex theories of hermeneutics, it is clearly and elegantly written.

Sleeper, C. F. "The Use of Scripture in Church Social Policy Statements." *Theology and Public Policy* 2 (1990): 47–60. A helpful essay by a well-known ethician, with important cautions about the use of biblical material.

*Spohn, W. S. *What Are They Saying About Scripture and Ethics?* New York/Ramsey: Paulist, 1984. Presently out of print; it will be reissued in revised form.

+ ———. *Go and Do Likewise: Jesus and Ethics*. New York: Continuum, 1999. One of the best works available for showing how Scripture influences and forms Christian ethics. Combines fine exegesis with theological sophistication.

Stackhouse, Max L. "Jesus and Economics: A Century of Reflection." In J. T. Johnson, ed. *The Bible in American Law, Politics and Political Rhetoric*, 107–52. Chico, Cal.: Scholars Press, 1985. An important survey of the use of the Bible for social reform, written mainly by Protestant scholars (for example, Walter Rauschenbusch and Shailer Matthews); it shows that many trends in contemporary Catholicism have historical precedent.

Wright, C. J. H. "The Use of the Bible in Social Ethics: Paradigms, Types and Eschatology." *Transformation* 1 (1984): 11–20.

▶   ◀

Bibliography on Preaching, Other Ministries of the Word, and Liturgy

My comments here overlap with John Baldovin's volume in this same series of *Studies in the Spirituality of Jesuits*, "Christian Liturgy: An Annotated Bibliography for Jesuits," 25, no. 5 (Nov. 1993). Baldovin calls attention to the important bibliographical essay by Mark Searle, "Liturgy and Social Ethics,: An Annotated Bibliography." *Studia Liturgica* 21 (1991): 220–335.

Achtemeier, Elizabeth. *The Old Testament and the Proclamation of the Gospel*. Philadelphia: Westminster Press, 1973. Though not specifically on issues of social justice, it contains helpful guidelines for use of OT.

Baldovin, John F. "The Liturgical Year: Calendar for a Just Community." In *Liturgy and Spirituality in Context*, ed. E. Bernstein, 98–114. Collegeville: Liturgical Press, 1990.

+ *Burghardt, Walter J. *When Christ Meets Christ. Homilies on the Just Word*. Mahwah, NJ: Paulist Press, 1993. Powerful examples of how to preach the just word.

———. *Preaching the Just Word*. New Haven: Yale University Press, 1996. Excellent work bringing together reflection on justice with great wisdom on how to preach about justice.

Burghardt, Walter, et al. "Preaching the Just Word: Resources for Homilists." *Homily Resources*. Special issue. Available from the Department of Social Development and World Peace of the U.S. Bishops' Conference. Essays on preaching and justice by Walter Burgardt, John Coleman, John Donahue, and James Connor. This volume is also available through the Woodstock Center.

*Empereur, James L., and Christopher Kiesling. *The Liturgy That Does Justice*. A Michael Glazier Book. Collegeville, Minn.: The Liturgical Press, 1990.

An excellent study with fine insights, covering all aspects of the liturgy. The annotated bibliography is worth the price of the book and should be consulted as a supplement to the present brief bibliography.

Gonzalez, J. L., and C. G. Gonzalez. *Liberation Preaching: The Bible and the Oppressed.* Nashville: Abingdon, 1980. Some good suggestions on preaching about social justice.

Grosz, Edward M., ed. *Liturgy and Social Justice: Celebrating Rites—Proclaiming Rights.* Collegeville: Liturgical Press, 1988. Papers read at the 1988 meeting of the Federation of Diocesan Liturgical Commissions. See especially Dianne Bergant, "Liturgy and Scripture: Creating a New World," 12–25, and J. Bryan Hehir, "Liturgy and Social Justice: Past Relationships and Future Possibilities," 40–61.

Guroian, V. "Bible and Ethics: An Ecclesial and Liturgical Interpretation. *Journal of Religious Ethics* 18 (1990): 129–57. Written from an Orthodox perspective, this essay offers interesting suggestions on the Bible, liturgy, and social justice, using examples from John Chrysostom.

+ Hamm, Dennis. *Preaching Biblical Justice: To Nurture the Faith That Does It. Studies in the Spirituality of the Jesuits* 29, no. 1 (Jan. 1997). Good brief discussion of justice, along with suggestions on preaching, with some sample homilies.

Hessel, Dieter, ed. *Social Themes of the Christian Year: A Commentary on the Lectionary.* Philadelphia: Geneva Press, 1983. A collection of essays on the lectionary cycle. Most helpful as a way to think differently about biblical texts, though the specific applications are uneven. Available through Westminster/John Knox Press.

Hughes, Kathleen, and Mark R. Francis, eds. *Living No Longer for Ourselves: Liturgy and Justice in the Nineties.* Collegeville, Minn.: The Liturgical Press, 1991. A good collection of essays. See especially Hughes, "Liturgy and Justice: An Intrinsic Relationship," 36–51, and R. A. Kiefer, "Liturgy and Ethics: Some Unresolved Dilemmas," 68–83.

Searle, Mark, ed. *Liturgy and Social Justice.* Collegeville, Minn.: The Liturgical Press, 1980. Important essays by Burghardt ("Preaching the Just Word"), Searle, Kilmartin, and Duffy.

+ Silberman, Lou H. "Boldness in the Service of Justice," In *Preaching Biblical Texts: Expositions by Jewish and Christian Scholars,* ed. Frederick C. Holmgren and Hermann E. Schaalmann, 29–35. Grand Rapids: Eerdmans, 1995.

Weakland, Rembert G. "Liturgy and Social Justice." In *Shaping the English Liturgy,* ed. P. Finn and J. Schellman, 343–57. Pastoral Press, 1990.

Wolterstorff, Nicholas P. "Justice as a Condition of Authentic Liturgy." *Theology Today* 48 (1991): 6–21.

Feminist Exegesis and Hermeneutics

One of the areas that have posed a major challenge to issues of faith and justice is the rise of feminism and the realization of the injustices to which women have been and are still subjected in both church and society. GC 34 called on Jesuits to listen to women's experience and to support movements for the liberation of women (d. 14, no. 12). Familiarity with feminist studies of the NT is one way to fulfill the mandate of the Congregation. While feminism (more recently designating itself "womanism") has spawned most fruitful research in countless areas—for example, literature, sociology, psychology, and all the branches of theology—feminist biblical scholars have been in the forefront in calling attention to the forgotten or suppressed history of women in the texts themselves and to the need for a feminist hermeneutics of texts and traditions. Carolyn Osiek, R.S.C.J., a professor of New Testament at the Catholic Theological Union, describes feminist interpretation in its broadest sense "as a concern for the promotion and dignity of women in all aspects of society, and in this context especially inasmuch as that promotion and dignity are conditioned by biblical interpretation" ("The Feminist and the Bible," 100); she offers as well an excellent overview of the different feminist approaches to the Bible. I will list works that fill out the picture she presents. (For further works in addition to these, see Trible, p. 17 above, and Schneiders, p. 64 above.)

▶   ◀

Bibliography on Feminist Hermeneutics

Anderson, Janice Capel. "Mapping Feminist Biblical Criticism: The American Scene 1983–90." In *Critical Review of Books in Religion*, 21–44. 1991. An excellent survey of both feminist theory and application to biblical texts.

Farley, Margaret. "Feminist Consciousness and the Interpretation of Scripture." In *Feminist Interpretation of the Bible,* ed. Letty Russell, 41–51. Philadelphia: Westminster, 1985.

Lindboe, I. M. "Recent Literature: Development and Perspectives in New Testament Research on Women." *Studia Theologica* 43 (1989): 153–63.

+Newsom, Carol A. and Sharon Ringe, eds. *Women's Bible Commentary*. Louisville: Westminster John Knox, 1998. Comments on individual books drawing on insights of feminist hermeneutics.

+Richter Reimer, Ivoni. *Women in the Acts of the Apostles: A Feminist Liberation Perspective*. Minneapolis, Minn.: Fotress, 1995.

Osiek, Carolyn, R.S.C.J. "The Feminist and the Bible: Hermeneutical Alternatives." *Religion and Intellectual Life* 6, nos. 3 and 4 (1989): 96–109.

+Reid, Barbara E. *Choosing the Better Part: Women in the Gospel of Luke*. Collegeville, Minn.: Liturgical Press, 1996. Combines theoretical perspectives on liberation with fine study of particular texts.

Sakenfield, K. D. "Feminist Biblical Interpretation." *Theology Today* 46 (1989): 154–68.

*Schüssler Fiorenza, Elisabeth. *In Memory of Her: A Feminist Theological Construction of Christian Origins.* New York: Crossroad, 1983. This is the most significant historical and exegetical study of the NT, providing the basis for feminist interpretation.

———. *Bread Not Stone: The Challenge of Feminist Biblical Interpretation.* Boston: Beacon Press, 1984. A fine collection of essays showing how feminist biblical interpretation poses important challenges for biblical scholarship and Church life. For Schüssler Fiorenza's most recent statements on interpretation, see her introduction to the Apocalypse, p. 62 above.

Tolbert, Mary Ann. "Defining the Problem: The Bible and Feminist Hermeneutics." *Semeia* 28 (1983): 113–26.

The Intimate Connection between Peace and Justice

The principal biblical term for peace, *šālôm*, does not mean simply the absence of conflict but suggests wholeness, completeness, or health. For this reason, in certain important biblical texts, especially those describing the effect of the just use of royal power, or in eschatological expectations of a restored kingdom, peace and justice are closely linked; for example, "Justice will bring about peace; right will produce calm and security" (Isa. 32:17, in the New American Bible translation); "Kindness and truth shall meet; justice and peace shall kiss. Truth shall spring out of the earth and justice shall look down from heaven" (Ps. 85:11f.). See also Isa. 9:7, 60:17; Ps. 72:7. One legacy of the OT is that peace, the condition which prevails in a healthy society, can never exist apart from the quest for justice. Yet, sadly, in Western history the Bible has been invoked far more often to warrant violent attacks on perceived enemies than to foster true peace. Yet the command of Jesus to love enemies and his sayings against violent resistance to evil not only have inspired individuals and spawned prophetic communities who proclaim and live in fidelity to these commands, but they also challenge all readers of the Bible to assess their own acquiescence to hatred and violence.

▶ ◀

Select Bibliography on Peace

The potential bibliography is vast. See especially Swartley, p. 69 below for a comprehensive bibliography.

Cadoux, C. J. *The Early Christian Attitude to War.* New York: Seabury, 1919, 1982. An early and important historical study of the first three centuries.

Craige, Peter C. *The Problem of War in the Old Testament.* Grand Rapids: Eerdmans, 1978. A popular and readable treatment of difficult issues such as the "holy war."

Daly, Robert J. "New Testament and the Early Church." In *Non-Violence— Central to Christian Pacifism,* ed. J. T. Culliton, 34–62. New York and Toronto: Edward Mellen Press. A good essay on the NT; the whole volume is recommended.

———. "The New Testament, Pacifism and Non-violence." *American Ecclesiastical Review* 168 (1974): 544–62. A good overview of important texts.

Harnack, Adolf. *Militia Christi: The Christian Religion and the Military in the First Three Centuries.* Philadelphia: Fortress, 1905, 1981. An important study of original sources for the relation of Christians to the military.

Hengel, Martin. *Victory over Violence: Jesus and the Revolutionists.* Philadelphia: Fortress, 1973. A careful historical study of the relation of Jesus to the revolutionary movements of his time.

Hirsch, R. G. *The Most Precious Gift: Judaism in Pursuit of Peace.* New York: Union of Hebrew Congregations, 1974. An excellent description of peace in Judaism.

*Klassen, William. *Love Your Enemies: The Way to Peace.* Philadelphia: Fortress, 1984. An excellent study of the love of enemies in Hellenistic and Jewish thought as well as in the NT. Excellent bibliography. .

McSorley, Richard. *The New Testament Basis of Peacemaking.* 3rd ed. rev. and expanded. Scottdale, Pa.: Herald Press, 1985. A good overview of pertinent texts; excellent for a parish or lay group.

Melko, Matthew, and Richard Weigel. *Peace in the Ancient World.* Jefferson, N.C.: McFarland and Co., 1981. Written by historians, this book studies a number of ancient societies that had sustained periods of peace, and it attempts to assess the political and social conditions that brought this about.

Perkins, Pheme. *Love Commands in the New Testament.* See p. 45 above.

Piper, John. *Love Your Enemies: Jesus' Love Command in the Synoptic Gospels and the Early Christian Paranesis.* Society for New Testament Studies Monograph Series, no. 38. Cambridge: Cambridge University Press, 1979. An excellent scholarly study of the literary setting of the love command.

Schottroff, Luise. "Non-Violence and the Love of Enemies." See p. 46 above.

*Swartley, Willard M., *Slavery, Sabbath, War and Women.* Scottdale, Pa.: Herald Press, 1983. Chap. 3, "The Bible and War," is one of the best treatments available. This work also contains comprehensive bibliographies on the issues covered.

———. ed. *The Love of Enemy and Nonretaliation in the New Testament.* Louisville: Westminster/John Knox Press, 1992. An excellent collection of essays on love of enemies and nonviolence, including a fine bibliography. See especially William Klassen, "Love Your Enemies: Current Status of Research"; Walter Wink, "Neither Passivity nor Violence: Jesus' Third

Way (Matt. 5:38–42)"; John R. Donahue, "Who Is My Enemy? The Parable of the Good Samaritan and the Love of Enemies."

Wengst, Klaus. *Pax Romana and the Peace of Jesus Christ.* Trans. by John Bowden. Philadelphia: Fortress, 1987. An outstanding scholarly and historical study of the ways in which Rome maintained its power and Christians offered nonviolent resistance to it.

Yoder, John H. *The Politics of Jesus.* Grand Rapids: Eerdmans, 1972. Perhaps the most influential book in recent decades on Jesus' relation to political issues, with a clear affirmation of nonviolence.

Zampaglione, G. *The Idea of Peace in Antiquity.* Notre Dame, Ind.: University of Notre Dame Press, 1973. A good collection of primary sources, but with little critical reflection.

Contextual Theology and Some More Recent Developments in Biblical Studies

Over the last decade, an array of new approaches to biblical material and to questions of justice has emerged, stimulated by the awaress of new contexts for theological reflection and biblical exegesis, the impact of globalization, as well as the need to "hear the voices from the margin." GC 34 showed an awareness of these challenges in discussing the impact of postmodernism on Jesuit life and on our need to have a "mission to culture," in its concern for interreligious dialogue, and especially in its call to a solidarity with people who lack power and resources; this concern has resulted in our ministering **to** and **with** them, while learning **from** them. I can offer neither a coherent summary of these new approaches, merging the lines between literary criticism, cultural criticism, biblical interpretation and theology, nor provide a comprehensive bibliography. Listed below are works that I and others have found to be especially helpful in securing a foundation for future work. The bibliography will focus on two major areas, Globalization and Contextual Theology, and "Postcolonial" criticism.

Globalization and Contextual Theology

I will list four works providing a fine introduction to the issues involved, followed by works dealing more directly with biblical material. Bevans (see below) defines contextual theology as "a way of doing theology in which one takes into acccount the spirit and message of the gospel; the tradition of the Christian people; the culture in which one is theologizing; and social change in that culture, whether brought about by western technological process or the grass-roots struggle for equality, justice and liberation" (*Models,* p. 1). Contextual theology can be a seen as an extension of "reading the signs of the times," and affirms that theological reflection, including biblical exegesis and pastoral practice, must be constantly aware of its own context, must listed to questions arising from the context of those addressed, and study the relation of these contexts to larger cultural and social interactions. In a global context it also involves an awareness that God's self-disclosure is found in the relgious experience of other cultures, so that discourse about the meaning of the Bible becomes dialogue rather than a one-sided communication.

▶   ◀

Bibliography on Globalization and Contextual Theology

+ Bevans, Stephen B. *Models of Contextual Theology.* Maryknoll, N.Y.: Orbis, 1992. Both Bevans and Schreiter teach at the Catholic Theological Union in Chicago.

+ Friedman, Thomas L. *The Lexus and the Olive Tree.* New York: Farrer, Straus, Giroux, 1999. Recommended by Sanks (see below) as an excellet popular introduction to globalization.

+ Schreiter, Robert. *Constructing Local Theologies.* Maryknoll, N.Y.: Orbis, 1994.

+ ———. *The New Catholicity: Theology between the Global and the Local.* Maryknoll, N.Y.: Orbis, 1998. Learned, comprehensive and very readable. This may be the best overview of the complex issues involved.

+ Said, Edward. *Orientalism.* New York: Random House, 1979. Seminal work in which Said points out how pictures of non-Western people are constructions and projections of Western values rather than accurate descriptions.

+ Sanks, T. Howland. "Globalization and the Church's Social Mission." *Theological Studies* 60 (4, 1999) 624–51. While focusing on the Church's social mission, Sanks provides a fine overview of the issues arising from globalization, as well as excellent bibliographical resources. See also the excellent article in *America* (Dec. 4, 1999), "Tales of Globalization," by William Boyle.

Biblical Studies

+ Bhabha, Homi K. "Postcolonial Criticism." In Stephen Greenblatt and Giles Gunn, eds. *Redrawing the Boundaries: The Transformation of English and American Literary Studies,* 437–65. New York: Modern Language Association of America, 1992. Bhabha is one of the most important theorists of postcolonial cultural studies and is now extensively consulted by biblical scholars. His major work is *The Location of Culture* (London: Routledge, 1994).

+ A. R. Crollius, ed. *Bible and Inculturation.* Working Papers on Living Faith and Cultures, III. Rome: Gregorian University Press, 1983. Four studies on the relation of particular biblical texts and themes to cultural situations.

+ Liew, Tat-siong Benny. *Politics of Parousia: Reading Mark Inter(con)textually.* Leiden: Brill, 1999. The chapters on method provide a good introduction to contemporary issues of "postcolonial" exegesis, while the interpretation of Mark is less enlightening.

+ Segovia, Fernando F., and Mary Ann Tolbert, eds. *Readings from This Place:* vol. 1: *Social Location and Biblical Interpretation in the United States;* vol. 2: *Social Location and Biblical Interpretation in Global Perspective.* Minneapolis: Fortress, 1995. An excellent collection of essays offering a methodological discussion of the impact that globalization and other points of view of exerted on biblical studies; it also includes representative essays by authors from global social locations.

+ ———. *Teaching the Bible: The Discourses and Politics of Biblical Pedagogy.* Maryknoll, N.Y.: Orbis, 1998. The author continues the approaches characteristic of the above volumes. Especially helpful are Segovia, "Pedagogical Discourse and Practices in Contemporary Biblical Criticism"; id., "Pedagogical Discourse and Practices in Cultural Studies: Toward Contextual Biblical Pedagogy; Joseph Hough, "Globalization in Theological Education"; and Tolbert, "A New Teaching With Authority: A Re-evaluation of the Authority of the Bible."

+ Sugirtharajah, R. S., ed. *The Postcolonial Bible.* Sheffield, Eng.: Sheffield Academic Press, 1998. A collection of essays exploring postcolonial appproaches. After teaching at different theological colleges in India Sugirtharajah is now lecturer in Third World Theologies at Selly Oak Colleges, Birmingham, England. He has emerged as a leading figure in joining postcolonial studies to theological reflection.

+ ———. "The Texts and the Texts: Use of the Bible in a multi-faith Context." In A. Lande and W. Ustorf, eds. *Mission in a Pluralistic World.* Frankfurt: Peter Lang, 1996.

+ ———. ed. *Voices from the Margin: Interpreting the Bible in the Third World.* Maryknoll: Orbis, 1991. Collection of interesting, indivdual studies by international authors, mainly from non first-world countries.

CONCLUDING REFLECTION

There is a sobering aspect to a survey such as this. Karl Barth once wrote: "The question, What is within the Bible? has a mortifying way of converting itself into the opposing question, Well, what are you looking for, and who are you, pray, who make bold to look?"⁵ We boldly look into the Bible from the perspective of prosperous, middle-class citizens of the United States. And yet the Bible summons its readers to a hermeneutics of suspicion of the culture in which they live. The Bible images a "contrast society." Can we face the contrast between the ideals presented by the Bible and life in our nation today or even in our "least Society"?

It is most important to note—and not stressed enough in this survey—that the Bible is at root not an ethical document, but the proclamation of the gracious love of God manifest for Christians in the Christ event. The gift precedes the demand: good news comes before good advice. For the Bible to be effective in social or individual ethics, we must have been captured by its saving message and have experienced the power of God's Spirit at work behind the written word. Apropos of the love command, Thomas Merton once expressed this well:

> The beginning of the fight against hatred, the basic Christian answer to hatred, is not the commandment to love, but what must necessarily come before in order to make the commandment bearable and comprehensible. It is a prior commandment *to believe*. The root of Christian love is not the will to love, but *the faith that one is loved*. The faith that one is loved *by God*. That faith that one is loved by God although unworthy or rather irrespective of one's worth!⁶

To do justice and walk humbly with our God ultimately proceeds from a deep experience of faith and conversion that is at the heart of the Spiritual Exercises and of Jesuit spirituality in every generation.

AN AFTERWORD

One of my hopes in offering such a survey is that readers will say, "Why didn't he mention this or that work, which I found very helpful?" In revising this I am grateful to those who offered suggestions and especially to colleagues at the Jesuit School of Theology at Berkeley. I would appreciate it very much if additions, criticisms, and suggestions could be sent directly to me at the Jesuit School of Theology at Berkeley, 1735 LeRoy Ave; Berkeley, CA 94709; e-mail: <jdonahue@jstb.edu>.

---

⁵ *The Word of God and the Word of Man* (New York and Evanston: Harper and Row, 1957), 32.

⁶ *A Thomas Merton Reader*, T. P. McDonnell, ed. (Doubleday: Image Books, 1974), 322, quoting from Merton's *New Seeds of Contemplation*.

APPENDIX
WHERE CAN I FIND THE BOOKS?

I have listed a large number of books and articles that I hope will send people scurrying to libraries and bookstores. I will list below some addresses, so those who might not have immediate access to a bookstore can contact the publishers directly. People might also want to write for catalogues, which is a fine way of keep abreast of issues. Some of these publishers have branch bookstores in many cities. Addresses and phone numbers have changed from the first edition of this bibliography, and I have added below also the web sites for various publishers. Many books can be ordered through www.amazon.com, www.barnesandnoble.com and www.kaboombooks.com (special for academic books).

Abingdon Press
201 Eighth Ave. South
P.O. Box 801
Nashville, TN 37202–0801
(800) 251–3320
http://www.abingdon.org

Augsburg Fortress Publishers
426 S. Fifth St., Box 1209
Minneapolis, MN 55440–1209
(800) 328–4648
http://www.augsburgfortress.org

Doubleday Publishers
1540 Broadway.
New York, NY 10036
http://www.bdd.com

The Crossroad Publishing Co.
370 Lexington Ave.
New York, NY 10017
(800) 937–5557
Crossroad Publishing Company
http://www.nbnbooks.com

Wm. B. Eerdmans Publ. Co.
255 Jefferson Ave, S.E.
Grand Rapids, MI 49503
(800) 253–7521.

Liturgical Press
St. John's Abbey
Collegeville, MN 56321
(612) 363–2213
http://www.litpress.org

Orbis Books
Maryknoll, NY 10545
(800) 258–5838
http://www.orbisbooks.com

Paulist Press
997 Macarthur Blvd
Mahwah, NJ 07430
(201) 825–7300
http://www.paulistpress.com

Westminster/John Knox Press
100 Witherspoon St.
Louisville, KY 40202–1396
(800) 523–1631
http://www.wjk.org

INDEX OF AUTHORS